Feb 2000

Happy
Birthday
Mom!
I hope your day
is as wonderful as you
are. I'm thinking of you!
Love
Anne Marie

MODERN JAPANESE COOKING AT HOME

神田川俊郎

TOSHIRO KANDAGAWA

OVERSEAS DISTRIBUTORS

UNITED STATES: JP TRADING, INC.

300 Industrial Way

Brisbane, Calif. 94005

Phone: (415)468-0775, 0776 Fax: (415)469-8038

MEXICO: Publicaciones Sayrols, S. A. de C. V.

COLOMBIA: Jorge E. Morales & CIA. LTDA.

TAIWAN: Formosan Magazine Press, Ltd.

HONG KONG: Apollo Book Company, Ltd.

THAILAND: Central Books Distribution, Co., Ltd.

SINGAPORE: MPH DISTRIBUTORS (S) PTE, LTD.

MALAYSIA: MPH DISTRIBUTORS SDN, BHD.

PHILIPPINES: National Book Store, Inc.

KOREA: Tongjin Chulpan Muyeok Co., Ltd.

INDONESIA: C. V. TOKO BUKU "MENTENG"

INDIA: Dani Book Land, Bombay 14

AUSTRALIA: BOOKWISE INTERNATIONAL

GUAM, SIPAN AND MICRONESIAN ISLANDS: FUJIWARA'S SALES & SERVICE

CANADA: MILESTONE PUBLICATIONS

U. S.A.:   MASA T. & ASSOCIATES

D & BH ENTERPRISE

First Edition 1997, 2nd Printing January 1998

Original Copyright © 1997 by Toshiro Kandagawa and Kazuo Mizutani

World rights reserved by JOIE, INC. 1-8-3, Hirakawa-cho, Chiyoda-ku, Tokyo 102 Japan;   Printed in Japan.

ISBN4-915831-82-5

INTRODUCTION

On Japanese dining tables, you can find dishes from many cultures, such as, Western, Chinese, Thai, and Indian, not to mention, Japanese. Any food can be obtained regardless of the season or the country of origin.

However, we have realized that old-fashioned Japanese meals are surprisingly healthy and were created to make the changing seasons by using the foods that are ripe and abundant at various times of the year. I would like to introduce a variety of dishes, from the traditional recipes to the Westernized one, which will help you provide an everchanging table.

I always try to serve customers with the most delicious dishes I can make. The principles of home cooking stay the same from generation to generation and can be summed up with my motto; "A little attention to detail results in a great taste."

Toshiro Kandagawa

BASIC COOKING INFORMATION

Today many areas of the world use the metric system and more will follow in the future. The following conversion tables are intended to serve as a guide to help you.

General points of information that may prove valuable or of interest:

1 Japanese cup = 200ml

1 American cup = 240ml = 8 American fl oz

1 British cup = 200ml = 7 British fl oz

1 tablespoon = 15ml   1 teaspoon = 5ml

TABLES CONVERTING FROM U.S. CUSTOMARY SYSTEM TO METRICS

Liquid Measures

U.S. Customary system	oz	g	ml
$\frac{1}{16}$ cup = 1T	$\frac{1}{2}$ oz	14g	15ml
$\frac{1}{4}$ cup = 4T	2 oz	60g	59ml
$\frac{1}{2}$ cup = 8T	4 oz	115g	118ml
1 cup = 16T	8 oz	225g	236ml
1 $\frac{3}{4}$ cups	14 oz	400g	414ml
2 cups = 1 pint	16 oz	450g	473ml
3 cups	24 oz	685g	710ml
4 cups	32 oz	900g	946ml

Liquid Measures

Japanese system	oz	ml
$\frac{1}{8}$ cup	$\frac{7}{8}$ oz	25ml
$\frac{1}{4}$ cup	1$\frac{3}{4}$ oz	50ml
$\frac{1}{2}$ cup	3$\frac{1}{2}$ oz	100ml
1 cup	7 oz	200ml
1$\frac{1}{2}$ cups	10$\frac{1}{2}$ oz	300ml
2 cups	14 oz	400ml
3 cups	21 oz	600ml
4 cups	28 oz	800ml

Weights   grams × 0.035 = ounces   ounces × 28.35 = grams

ounces to grams	grams to ounces
$\frac{1}{4}$ oz = 7g	1g = 0.035 oz
$\frac{1}{2}$ oz = 14g	5g = $\frac{1}{6}$ oz
1 oz = 30g	10g = $\frac{1}{3}$ oz
2 oz = 60g	28g = 1 oz
4 oz = 115g	100g = 3$\frac{1}{2}$ oz
6 oz = 170g	200g = 7 oz
8 oz = 225g	500g = 18 oz
16 oz = 450g	1000g = 35 oz

*Equivalent

Linear Measures   inches × 2.54 = centimeters   centimeters × 0.39 = inches   in = inch(es)   cm = centimeter(s)

inches to centimeters	centimeters to inches
$\frac{1}{2}$ in = 1.27 cm	1 cm = $\frac{3}{8}$ in
1 in = 2.54 cm	2 cm = $\frac{3}{4}$ in
2 in = 5.08 cm	3 cm = 1$\frac{1}{8}$ in
4 in = 10.16 cm	4 cm = 1$\frac{1}{2}$ in
5 in = 12.7 cm	5 cm = 2 in
10 in = 25.4 cm	10 cm = 4 in
15 in = 38.1 cm	15 cm = 5$\frac{3}{4}$ in
20 in = 50.8 cm	20 cm = 8 in

The water boiling temperature given is at sea level.

Conversion factors:

$$C = (F - 32) \times \frac{5}{9}$$

$$F = \frac{C \times 9}{5} + 32$$

C = Celsius   F = Fahrenheit

Temperatures

Fahrenheit (F) to Celsius (C)	Celsius (C) to Fahrenheit (F)
freezer storage −10°F = −23.3°C	freezer storage −20°C = −4°F
0°F = −17.7°C	−10°C = 14°F
water freezes 32°F = 0 °C	water freezes 0°C = 32°F
68°F = 20 °C	10°C = 50°F
100°F = 37.7°C	50°C = 122°F
water boils 212°F = 100 °C	water boils 100°C = 212°F
300°F = 148.8°C	150°C = 302°F
400°F = 204.4°C	200°C = 392°F

Deep-Frying Oil Temperatures

300°F − 330°F(150°C − 165°C) = low	
340°F − 350°F(170°C − 175°C) = moderate	
350°F − 360°F(175°C − 180°C) = high	

Oven Temperatures

250°F − 350°F(120°C − 175°C) = low or cool	
350°F − 400°F(175°C − 204°C) = moderate or medium	
400°F − 450°F(204°C − 230°C) = hot	
450°F − 500°F(230°C − 260°C) = very hot	

Toshiro Kandagawa's
MODERN JAPANESE COOKING AT HOME

KANDAGAWA HONTEN

Loved for its authentic but original Japanese dishes, Kandagawa Honten uses the freshest seasonal ingredients, and the owner's spirit for culinary art can be seen in his drawings on the placemats or on the chopstick wrappers. Casual counters on the first floor, *tatami* rooms on the second.

Address: 1-2-25, Dojima, Kita-ku, Osaka phone : 06-341-7862

Open Monday to Saturday, 16:00-1:00 Price of full-course meal: ￥23,000 and up

Other branches:

AJI KANDAGAWA phone: 06-346-1980   SETSUGETSUKA KANDAGAWA phone: 06-343-0656

AJIHUUGETSU KANDAGAWA phone:06-345-0737   NEW FRANCE KAISEKI KANDAGAWA phone: 06-345-4682

Toshiro Kandagawa

About the AUTHOR

Toshiro Kandagawa was born in Kyoto, the former location of the capital of Japan. When he was sixteen he determined to become a cook and began his training at "Nadaman", known as one of the most traditional restaurants in Kyoto. Later, at the age of only twenty-two, he started his own business by opening a Japanese-style bistro. Then in 1965, he opened an authentic Japanese restaurant named "Kandagawa Honten", the main branch of the group at Kita-shinchi, Osaka. The reputation made quite a name for itself and its owner and soon he began to appear on TV and home magazines. On the other hand Kandagawa also devotes himself to teaching younger cooks and has opened several other branches.

CONTENTS

STAFF

Cooking Assistants : Tokuo Endo
Koichi Taniguchi
Jinichi Tateyama
Naoto Iino
Keisuke Tamano
Hisato Sakane
Photographers : Yoshikatsu Saeki
Fumiko Sugawara
Cover Design : Manabu Chinan
Text Layout : Mayumi Shinohara
Table Coordinator : Megumi Yamaki
Text : Keiko Takahashi
Translator : Yoko Ishiguro

Project Editor : Kazuo Mizutani

Notes:
◆ Each recipe serves 4, but the photograph of the completed dish may contain only 1 serving.
◆ The asterisks (★) next to the process photographs indicate an important point in the cooking.

COOKING BASICS

In Japanese cooking, preparation of each ingredient is the key to success.

Do not hesitate to devote your time and effort to this preparation for it will result in the best taste. As long as you hold to the basics, the final taste will be as good as you can imagine even if you skip on later steps. Practice my saying: A little attention to detail will result in a surprisingly delicious dish. Another key point is to put your heart into pleasing your family or guests.

KANDAGAWA'S MODERN JAPANESE COOKING AT HOME

PREPARATION OF SEAFOOD

How to cut fish into fillets

❶Remove head.

❷Slice off the sharp scales near the tail.

❸Slice off upper fillet by holding near the tail inserting knife from the same end, and sliding along the bone.

❹Turn over and slice off the other fillet in the same manner.

❺Two fillets are now ready to be used.

How to remove fish odor

This is a simple but effective technique to freshen the flavor of seafood before actual cooking such as simmering. In Japan, it is called "hoarfrost" as the surface of treated seafood resembles delicate frost.

❶Sprinkle fish with rice wine and let stand for about 10 minutes. Blanch in boiling water.

❷Remove and plunge into ice water; wipe dry.

Deveining prawns

Do not skip this process or your prawns will have a fishy odor. Insert a skewer into the middle of back, and pull out dark vein. Shelling is not necessary to devein.

Scoring calamari

Decorative scores on calamari make it easier to hold the seasonings well when simmered or stir-fried. Remove skin before scoring.

❶Holding a knife at a slant, make fine scores at about 5mm (1/8") intervals in one direction.

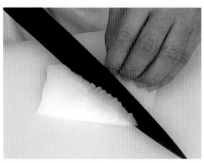

❷Turn the fillet around and make fine scores in the same manner crosswise. Cut into desired sizes.

PREPARATION OF VEGETABLES

Rubbing salt on cucumber

This is a good way to remove extra moisture and extract a definite flavor.

Place one or two cucumbers on a cutting board, sprinkle with a generous amount of salt and rub into cucumbers, rolling them back and forth.

Freshening lotus root and *udo*

Since lotus root and *udo* discolor quickly, they need a treatment before cooking.

Dilute 1 teaspoon vinegar in 400ml water and soak lotus root or *udo* in this vinegared water right after slicing. Let stand 10 minutes and rinse in water.

Blanching burdock

Uncooked vegetables for salad should be blanched in cold water to increase crispness. Some vegetables with harsh or bitter taste need to be blanched as well.

Plunge burdock into water as you cut into pieces to remove bitterness and to prevent discoloring.

Rounding off corners

When simmering *daikon* radish, pumpkin or any vegetable that is fragile when cooked, cut off corners of the cut pieces to retain shape.

Cut pumpkin into desired size, peel partially, and scrape off corners.

Hexagonal peeling of taro

This is another kind of rounding off especially for simmering taro.

Cut off the top and bottom of taro, then peel the sides along the curve to make six even sides.

OTHER PREPARATIONS

Preparing *abura-age* (deep-fried *tofu* pouches)

This process is necessary to remove the oily smell and to let fried *tofu* absorb seasonings easily.

Bring water to a boil in a pot and cook *abura-age* briefly in it, or lay *abura-age* in a colander and pour boiling water over them; drain.

Softening dried *shiitake*

Drying *shiitake* mushroom increases its flavor, it is therefore preferred for simmered or braised dishes to fresh ones. The water in which *shiitake* was soaked is a good vegetable *dashi* stock

In a small container, place a pinch of sugar and pour lukewarm water enough to cover the mushrooms, and soak them with a light weight or covered 30 minutes to 2 hours until soft.

APPETIZERS & SASHIMI

Serve *sashimi* with a difference. Various *aemono*, or dressed foods, are introduced here as appetizers or good rice companions.

SASHIMI SALAD WITH HERBS

Fish au naturel with tansy plum
dressing and abundant condiments

Ingredients : 4 servings

200 g (7 oz) fresh sea bream for *sashimi*	**Plum dressing**
	40g (1 1/2 oz) pickled plums
3 sprouts *myoga* (Zingiber mioga)	50ml *kombu* stock
	2 tablespoons rice vinegar
1/2 small cucumber	2 teaspoons light soy sauce
50g (1 3/4 oz) carrot	
5 beefsteak leaves (*shiso*)	4 teaspoons *mirin* (see page 102)
50g (1 3/4 oz) mountain yam (*nagaimo*)	4 tablespoons vegetable oil
20g (2/3 oz) salted *kombu* kelp	Pinch toasted sesame seeds
Few sprigs beefsteak plant florets (optional)	

Method

Make plum dressing

❶ Remove stones from pickled plums. Using a knife, mince until smooth. Place in a bowl and mix with other dressing ingredients.

Prepare condiments

❷ Slice *myoga* finely and soak in water to remove harshness. Peel and cut cucumber and carrot, then cut into 2-3" lengths. Using the *katsuramuki* technique(A), thinly "peel" and shred the carrot and cucumber diagonally. Wind the threads around a chopstick to form a spiral and soak in cold water (C-D). Cut beefsteak leaves into 5mm(1/8") squares. Cut mountain yam into rectangles. Shred salted *kombu* kelp.

Make sea bream *sashimi*

❸ Slice sea bream fillet thinly, using a knife almost horizontally, and arrange on a platter (E-F). Arrange condiments and beefsteak sprigs to please the eye. Sprinkle with plum dressing.

Professional Hints

If you have time, marinate the fish fillet by wrapping with *kombu* kelp for 4 hours before adding dressing. Any fresh fish can served in the same way.

A

Katsuramuki: "Peel" 2" (5cm) long carrot into a paper-thin sheet.

B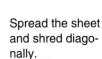

Spread the sheet and shred diagonally.

C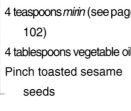

Wind the shreds around cooking chopstick to make a curl. This makes a charming decoration on the plate.

★ D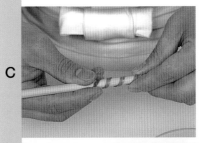

Remove chopsticks gently and soak in cold water to freshen. Prepare cucumber shreds in the same manner.

E

Always hold the fillet with your left hand while slicing diagonally.

F

Arrange on a platter in whirls, starting at the sides, overlapping each slightly with the next.

DRIED RADISH SALAD

Chicken and vegetable salad enhanced with aromatic sesame dressing.

Ingredients: 4 servings

40g (1 1/3 oz) dried *daikon* radish, soaked in water

200g (7 oz) chicken thigh, cut into bite-sizes

1 tablespoon vegetable oil

Salt and pepper

1/2 small cucumber (1/4 Western cucumber)

1/3 cake *konnyaku* (see page 102)

50g (1 3/4 oz) carrot

Sesame dressing

- 6 tablespoons sesame paste
- 1 teaspoon minced ginger
- 1 teaspoon minced garlic
- 3 tablespoons minced green onion
- 50ml *dashi* stock (see page 96)
- 3 tablespoons soy sauce
- 3 tablespoons rice vinegar
- 2 tablespoons sugar
- Dash sesame chili oil

Crushed almonds

Radish

Method

Preparation

❶Drain dried *daikon* radish and parboil just until soft but still crunchy, about 30 minutes. Blanch in cold water (A) and squeeze out water.

❷In a pan, stir-fry chicken pieces with a little oil; season with salt and pepper.

❸Rub cucumber with salt until the surface becomes slightly bruised; cut into julienne strips. Cut *konnyaku* and carrot into the same size and shape, and parboil.

Combine

❶In a bowl, mix dressing ingredients (B). Add chicken and vegetables and toss well so the ingredients absorb the seasonings well.

❷Place in a serving dish and scatter with thinly sliced radish and crushed almonds.

★ A

B

Boil dried *daikon* radish only briefly; drain while they are still springy when pushed with fingers.

Sesame paste and soy sauce make the base of the dressing while garlic and chili oil add an accent.

Professional Hints

Be sure to parboil the vegetables so the moisture will not spoil the rich sesame dressing. Adjust the amount of sesame chili oil according to diners' taste.

PRAWNS WITH *WASABI* MAYONNAISE

**Mild mayonnaise and cream sauce is enhanced
with sharp *wasabi* horseradish.**

Ingredients: 4 servings

20 prawns

Batter

⌐ Salt and pepper
| 1 egg white
└ 3 tablespoons cornstarch

Oil for deep-frying

50g(1 3/4 oz) green beans

50g(1 3/4 oz) carrot

Pinch salt

Dressing

⌐ 6 tablespoons mayonnaise
| 4 tablespoons fresh cream
| Salt and pepper
| 1 tablespoon *wasabi*
| (see page 104)
| Pinch salt
└ 1 teaspoon rice vinegar

Chervil

A

Toss cooled prawns and well-drained vegetables with the dressing.

Method

Preparation

❶Shell and devein prawns. In a small bowl mix batter ingredients and dip each prawn. Deep-fry in 180℃(360°F) oil and drain.

❷Cut green beans into 3cm(1") lengths. Cut carrot into the same length julienne strips. Cook briefly in salted boiling water; drain.

Mix

❸In a bowl, mix dressing ingredients. Add prawns and vegetables and combine well (A).

❹Serve garnished with chervil.

Professional Hints

Deep-fry prawns just until cooked. Do not brown the outside so the soft and fluffy coating will not be spoiled. For the same reason, toss with dressing just before serving.

SEAFOOD SALAD WITH MUSTARD-VINEGAR-*MISO*

**Fresh scallops, calamari and clams enhanced with
fragrant vegetables and flavorful white *miso* dressing.**

Ingredients: 4 servings

100g(7 oz)	fresh scallops	**Miso sauce**
100g(7 oz)	fresh calamari	
Dash rice wine		75g (2 1/4 oz) white *miso*
300g(10 1/2oz)	short-neck	1 tablespoon red barley *miso*
	clams or other shellfish	2 tablespoons rice wine
1 bunch scallion*(wakegi)*		3 tablespoons sugar
50g(1 3/4 oz)	*udo* (Aralia	1 egg yolk
	Cordata) or celery	2 tablespoons rice vinegar
50g(1 3/4 oz) carrot		Dash hot mustard
50g(1 3/4 oz)	lily bulb	Dash lemon juice
		Kinome(sansho sprouts, optional)

Method

Preparation

❶Cut scallops and calamari into bite-size pieces. Place in a pot, sprinkle rice wine and cook, constantly shaking the pot (A).

❷Boil short-neck clams and shell.

❸Boil scallion and blanch in ice cold water. On a cutting board, press out the jelly-like water inside using your fist (B).

❹Cut carrot and *udo* into thin rectangles. Boil them and drain. Peel off lily cloves and boil; drain.

Make mustard-vinegar-*miso* sauce

❺In a pot, combine *miso* sauce ingredients. Using a spatula, stir constantly for 5 minutes over low heat until smooth. When almost cooled, add vinegar, mustard and lemon juice. Blend well.

❻In a bowl, combine all ingredients with the sauce.

❼Place in individual serving bowl in a heap, and garnish with *sansho* sprouts.

Professional Hints

Be sure to cook the sauce over low heat as the egg yolk will scorch easily. This sauce keeps indefinitely to be used for other dishes such as minced meat, *furofuki*, or *dengaku*. Make a large portion and save for later uses.

Add vinegar and mustard at the final step to make the dressing pungent.

A
Cooking scallop and calamari in rice wine removes fish odor and extracts the aroma.

B
A rolling pin can be used to press out the jelly-like water from the green onion as well.

POTATO AND CALAMARI SALAD

**Japanese version of tasty potato salad
with cooked calamari and onion.**

Ingredients: 4 servings

2 potatoes
200g(7 oz) calamari
1/2 onion
1 tablespoon vegetable oil
2-3 stalks *asatsuki*(thin
green onion, optional)

Dressing

- 6 tablespoons
  mayonnaise
- 1 tablespoon whole
  grain mustard
- 1/3 lemon, squeezed

Professional Hints

Cook onion until soft to extract its sweetness whereas calamari should be cooked only briefly as it becomes too chewy if cooked well. Whole grain mustard will give a special flavor to this dish.

Method

Preparation

❶Cut potatoes into matchsticks(A) and boil for about 3 minutes; drain and allow to cool (B).

❷Cut calamari into the same size as potatoes. Shred onion. Cut green onion into 1cm(3/8 ") lengths.

Stir-fry

❸Heat vegetable oil in a pan, add onion and stir-fry until supple. Add calamari and briefly stir-fry (C).

Mix

❹In a bowl, combine dressing ingredients and add potatoes, onion and calamari. Mix well (D) and finally add green onion.

A

Cut potatoes into same size matchsticks.

B

To retain its own flavor, drain in a colander and let stand to cool(Do not plunge in cold water).

★
C

Stir-fry onion until very soft, then add calamari.

D

When potatoes, onion and calamari are cooled, combine with dressing ingredients.

BONITO *SASHIMI* WITH SPECIAL GREEN SAUCE

**The natural flavor of fresh bonito is enriched with special sauce
made of beafsteak leaves, anchovy and olive oil.**

Ingredients: 4 servings

1 fillet fresh bonito	3 tablespoons vegetable oil
Dash rice wine	1 teaspoon rice vinegar
Salt and pepper	1 1/2 teaspoons soy sauce
Green sauce	1 1/2 tablespoons lemon juice
25 beefsteak leaves *(shiso)*	1 teaspoon white wine
1 clove garlic	*Daikon* radish, optional
1 teaspoon capers	*Daikon* radish sprouts,
1 fillet anchovy	optional
3 tablespoons olive oil	Pinch sesame seeds, toasted

Method

Make green sauce
❶Grate the clove of garlic on the serrated walls of *grinding bowl*. Add minced beefsteak leaves and grind into a paste (A). Add remaining ingredients and blend well until smooth, using a whisk.

Prepare condiments
❷Shred *daikon* radish and carrot using *katsuramuki* technique (see page 100). Fill a bowl with cold water and soak *daikon* radish and sprouts until crisp.

Grill bonito
❸Trim away the dark part from bonito fillet. Sprinkle with rice wine and salt. Broil over high flame, preferably skewered, just until the outside is hardened and the inside stays succulent. Plunge into ice water (B) to prevent continued cooking, drain and pat-dry. Slice thinly and season with salt and pepper.

Arrange
❹On a large serving platter, arrange sliced bonito and pour over green dressing. Sprinkle with toasted sesame seeds and garnish with well-drained *daikon,* carrot and sprouts.

Professional Hints

The zesty blend of soy sauce, olive oil and beafsteak leaves improves any seafood or vegetable salads. Blend the ingredients quickly and vigorously just before serving so the beefsteak leaves do not lose its flavor.

A

Grind garlic and beefsteak leaves well to extract the flavor. (A blender or food processor can be used.)

★
B

Broiling and cooling processes give the bonito *sashimi* a delectable smoky flavor.

SUMMERY SALAD

Refreshing vegetable salad using all seasonal ingredients with spicy onion dressing.

Ingredients: 4 servings

2 medium tomatoes

2 Japanese eggplants or 1 American eggplant, peeled

Vegetable oil for deep-frying

1/2 red onion

1 package *daikon* radish sprouts

3 sprouts *myoga*

200g(7 oz) mountain yam*(nagaimo)*

Onion dressing

1/2 stalk green onion, minced

5 tablespoons soy sauce

50ml rice vinegar

50ml water

2 tablespoons sesame oil

1 tablespoon sugar

1 teaspoon minced garlic

1 teaspoon minced ginger

Red beefsteak plant sprouts, optional

Method

Preparation

❶Peel tomatoes: Dip in boiling water a few seconds and then quickly plunge into ice water. (A) This way tomatoes can be peeled smoothly with fingers. Cut into 5mm(1/5") thicknesses.

❷Cut eggplants into rolling wedges (see page 98) and deep-fry in 180℃ (360°F) oil.

❸Shred red onion and *myoga*, and soak them in cold water. Trim away roots of *daikon* radish sprouts. Peel mountain yam and cut into 5mm to 1 cm(1/5" to 3/8) cubes.

Arrangement

❹In a shallow dish, lay tomato and eggplant slices alternately. Top with remaining vegetables in a good color combination. Blend dressing ingredients (B) and pour over the salad. Top with beefsteak plant sprouts.

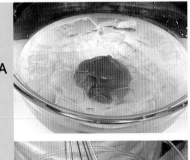

A

On top of each tomato, cut an 'X'. Dip in boiling water, then plunge into ice water to prevent cooking. Slip off skins.

B

Use abundant herbs such as ginger, garlic and green onion and stir well to blend the flavors.

PRAWNS AND EGGPLANTS WITH GREEN SAUCE

The fresh, young soy bean sauce compliments shrimp and eggplants in both color and flavor as another taste particular to summer.

Ingredients: 4 servings

12 prawns

4 eggplants (or 2 American
    eggplants)

Pinch salt

Green sauce

250g(9 oz) young soy beans in pod

120ml *dashi* stock (see page 96)

1 teaspoon light soy sauce

Pinch salt

Marinade for eggplants

180ml *dashi* stock

20ml light soy sauce

20ml *mirin* (see page 102)

1 teaspoon rice wine

Method

Make sauce

❶In a pot, bring ample water to a boil and cook soy bean pods with a pinch of salt until tender. Drain in a colander and sprinkle with salt.

❷When the pods are cooled, shell and remove the filmy skin of the beans. Place in a grinding bowl and grind roughly (A). Add *dashi*, light soy sauce and salt, and blend well.

Cook shrimp

❹Boil unshelled shrimp; drain, sprinkle with salt and set aside to cool. Shell.

Cook eggplants

❺In a pot, put marinade ingredients and bring to a boil; set aside.

❻Broil eggplants over high flame(B). When the inside is cooked and soft, plunge into cold water. Peel and pat dry. Add to the marinade and let stand about 3 hours.

Arrange

❼Lightly squeeze eggplants to remove extra moisture. In individual serving bowl, lay an eggplant and arrange shrimp over it. Drizzle green sauce over to be mixed to eat.

Do not grind until smooth. Leave some crunchiness to retain the flavor and color of young soy beans.

Broil eggplant over high flame turning over so the skin browns all around.Blanch in cold water for easy peeling.

18

MARINATED HERRING ROE

**Easy yet tasty dish to serve
with wine or rice.**

Ingredients: 4 servings

200g (1/2 lb) or 8 salted herring roes

Pinch salt

1/2 dried calamari *(surume)*

10g (1/3 oz) *kombu* kelp

Marinade

300ml *dashi* stock (see page 96)

2 tablespoons soy sauce

2 tablespoons light soy sauce

4 tablespoons *mirin*

2 tablespoons rice wine

Garnish

Daikon radish

Carrot

Method

Preparation

❶Soak herring roes in water to remove saltiness. A pinch of salt added to water will accelerate the process. Let stand 3-4 hours.

❷Broil dried calamari briefly to make the surface crisp. Using a pair of scissors, shred dried calamari and *kombu*.

❸Bring the marinade ingredients to a boil; allow to cool.

Marinate

❹Soak herring roe, calamari and *kombu* in the marinade and let stand at least an hour or preferably overnight.

Prepare garnish

❺Cut *daikon* and carrot into long julienne strips lengthwise. Boil until supple and make a knot as shown (B). Place marinated herring roe in a serving dish and top with bound vegetable strips.

★

A

B

Marinate at least an hour to blend the flavors of *kombu* and calamari.

Make a loop with each *daikon* and carrot strip. Put one loop into another and bring out the ends through the loop. In Japan red and white combination is used as a sign of celebration.

Professional Hints

Dissolve a pinch of salt in the soaking water. This way the roes will not completely lose the saltiness and let the marinade flavor penetrate easily.

19

CHICKEN SAUTÉED WITH *MENTAIKO* MAYONNAISE

Rich and spicy sauce enhances the plain flavored chicken dish.

Ingredients: 4 servings

1 or 300g (10 oz) chicken thigh

Salt and pepper

1/2 head broccoli, cooked

1 tablespoon vegetable oil

1/2 lemon, sliced

***Mentaiko* mayonnaise**

- 2 tablespoons *mentaiko* (chili cod roe)
- 2 tablespoons mayonnaise
- 1 egg yolk

Chervil

Method

Preparation

❶Cut chicken thigh into thin and narrow bite size pieces. Sprinkle with salt and pepper.

Sauté chicken

❷In a frying pan, heat vegetable oil until hot and sauté chicken pieces, skin sides first. Turn when beautifully browned.(A)

❸In a small bowl, blend skinned *mentaiko*, mayonnaise and egg yolk into a paste. Spoon this paste onto the meat side of chicken. Cover and cook (B).

❹Arrange chicken pieces on a serving plate and garnish with broccoli, lemon slices and chervil.

★ A

Cook chicken over high heat until browned in order to extract the flavor, then reduce heat to cook thoroughly.

B

Coat the meat sides of chicken with *mentaiko* mayonnaise and turn over to cook with remaining heat only, covered.

Professional Hints

Do not add *mentaiko* mayonnaise until both sides of chicken are browned. Keep the skin crisp. Egg yolk makes the sauce milder.

Method

Preparation

❶Cut chicken liver into bite-size pieces. Soak in milk to remove the odor (A). Drain and wash under running water; pat dry. Sprinkle with salt and pepper, and coat with cornstarch. Deep-fry in hot vegetable oil.

❷Rub cucumbers with salt to release extra moisture, and cut into 5cm(2") length julienne strips. Cut red bell pepper into julienne strips and parboil briefly.

❸Slice green onion thinly and soak in water to remove harshness.

Mix and serve

❹In a bowl combine dressing ingredients and drained green onion (B). Add liver and cucumber, and mix well (C).

❺Place in serving dish and top with dried bonito shavings.

Professional Hints

Marinating and deep-frying create a favorite dish for everyone who loves chicken liver. Adjust the amount of chili paste according to your taste. This Chinese dressing will go with other vegetable and meats. Enjoy variations.

A

Soak liver to remove unpleasant odor.

★ B

Blend dressing ingredients with sliced green onion and let stand a while so the onion absorb the flavor.

C

Add cucumber and mix well, then add fried liver.

CHICKEN LIVER AND CUCUMBER SALAD

Chili bean paste and sesame oil give a deep flavor to this excellent beer companion.

Ingredients: 4 servings

200g (7 oz) chicken livers
  Milk to soak livers in
4 small cucumbers
1 green onion
1/2 red bell pepper
  Salt and pepper
  Cornstarch for dusting
Vegetable oil for deep-frying
Dressing
⌈ 50ml soy sauce
  50ml rice vinegar
  50ml sesame oil
  1 1/2 tablespoons sugar
  Chili bean paste
⌊ Minced garlic
Dried bonito shavings

SHELLFISH AND VEGETABLE WITH GREEN VINEGAR

This refreshing sour sauce is a blend of *Tosa* vinegar and grated cucumbers.

Ingredients: 4 servings

2 small cucumbers

1/2 tablepoon cornstarch

Lemon juice

1/3 stalk *udo* (see page 104)

50g(1 3/4 oz) carrot

50g(1 3/4 oz) green beans

2 radishes

2 *myoga* sprouts

3 fresh ark shells

3 cockle shells

2 fresh *shiitake* mushrooms

Dash each rice wine,vinegar and salt

Tosa vinegar

- 90ml *dashi* stock
- 2 tablespoons light soy sauce
- 2 tablespoons *mirin*
- 2 tablespoon rice vinegar
- 3cm(1 1/8") square *kombu*
- Dried bonito shavings

Marinade

- 1 cup (200ml) *dashi* stock
- 20ml light soy sauce
- 20ml *mirin*
- Dash rice wine

Bind split cucumbers with an elastic and grate together for an even green hue.

Vegetables absorb *dashi* stock well if boiled to release extra moisture.

Professional Hints

Marinatiing gives a light but deep flavor to the vegetables. Enjoy variations using other shellfish or calamari.

Method

Make green vinegar

❶Rub cucumbers with salt until soft. Blanch in boiling water and then in cold water; wipe dry. Cut lengthwise in half and spoon out the seeds. Grate, binding cucumber sticks with elastic (A). Drain in a colander.

❷In a pot combine *Tosa* Vinegar ingredients and cornstarch, and heat stirring until thickened. Add lemon juice and let stand to cool. Mix with grated cucumbers.

Prepare vegetables and shellfish

❸In a pot bring marinade ingredients to a boil; let stand to cool. Peel *udo* and cut into 5cm(2") length julienne strips. Soak in vinegared water. Cut carrot and green beans into the same size strips. Boil vegetable strips (do not overcook *udo*); drain and place in the marinade(B).

❹Cut shellfish into small pieces. Sprinkle *shiitake* with salt and rice wine, and grill briefly; slice thinly.

❺Arrange vegetables and shellfish in a serving bowl. Garnish with sliced radish and *myoga*.

TOFU AND FIREFLY CALAMARI SALAD

Healthy *tofu* salad with ample vegetables. Aromatic *miso* dressing stimulates appetite.

Ingredients: 4 servings

1 cake *tofu*, drained

100g(3 1/2 oz) boiled firefly calamari

1/2 bunch rape seed flower

Pinch salt

1 tomato

5 bronze lettuce leaves

1/4 red onion

1/2 small cucumber

5cm(2") *daikon* radish

1/3 carrot

1/3 package *daikon* radish sprouts

Salted *kombu*, shredded

Kinome miso dressing

- 120ml vegetable oil
- 50ml rice vinegar
- 1 tablespoon soy sauce
- 2 tablespoons white *miso*
- 1 teaspoon whole grain mustard
- Salt and pepper
- 1/2 package *kinome*(young *sansho* leaves)
- 2 tablespoons minced onion

Method

Preparation

❶Slice *tofu* horizontally in half, then cut each into 10 equal pieces. Transfer onto a serving dish.

❷Remove eyes and cartilage from firefly calamari. Wash under running water.

❸Cook rape seed flowers in boiling water; drain and cut in half. Cut tomato into 2cm (1") cubes.

❹Tear lettuce into bite-size pieces. Slice red onion thinly and soak in cold water.

❺Shred cucumber, *daikon* and carrot. Discard root ends of *daikon* radish sprouts and toss with other vegetable shreds.

Serve

❻Place calamari and lettuce on *tofu*. Top with shredded vegetables and salted *kombu*. Blend dressing ingredients and pour over salad (B).

A

Toss vegetables before serving so that strips do not stick each other.

B

Loosen the consistency of *miso* stirring with other ingredients, then stir in minced onion and *kinome*.

Professional Hints

It is important to drain *tofu* well, or the whole dish will become watery. Although this is recommendable for spring when firefly calamari is in season, common calamari, shrimp, octopus can be good substitutes.

23

GRILLED DISHES & FRIED DISHES

Grilled or fried dishes need no complicated preparation, therefore they are ideal for everyday meals. Here you will find a wide range of them from a simple grilled fish to a fusion of international tastes. Try the Japanese cooking devices to use less oil.

EGGPLANT WITH BEEF-*MISO* STUFFING

Fun-to-look-at, delicious to taste *miso*-based stuffing sandwiched between
eggplant rounds. Pan-frying enhances the plain taste of eggplant.

Ingredients: 4 servings

2 *Kamo-nasu* or large eggplants

2 tablespoons vegetable oil

1 stalk green onion

2 *myoga* sprouts

1/2 package *daikon* radish sprouts

Miso stuffing

150g(5 1/4 oz) thinly sliced beef

1 package *shimeji* mushrooms

1/2 each red and yellow
   bell pepper

20 ginkgo nuts, toasted

4 tablespoons red barley *miso*

2 tablespoons *Haccho* or
   akadashi miso

1 teaspoon chili bean paste

5 tablespoons rice wine

3 tablespoons sugar

Grated garlic

Method

Fry eggplants

❶Cut eggplants into 2cm(3/4") rounds. Heat 1 tablespoon vegetable oil in a frying pan and fry eggplant slices (A). Set aside.

Make stuffing

❷Cut beef into 1cm(3/8") wide strips. Trim mushrooms and separate into segments. Seed bell peppers and cut into rolling wedges. Skin ginkgo nuts.

❸Heat 1 tablespoon oil in frying pan and stir-fry beef, mushrooms, ginkyo nuts and peppers until soft. Add remaining seasonings and stir until smooth on low heat.

Arrange and serve

❹Shred green onion and *myoga*, then soak in cold water. Trim *daikon* radish sprouts and cut in half.

❺In a shallow serving dish place a half amount of fried eggplant slices. Cover each slice with *miso* stuffing in a heap. Top with remaining slices of eggplant(B & C). Garnish with drained green onion, *myoga* and radish sprouts. Drizzle remaining *miso* stuffing.

Professional Hints

Blending two kinds of *miso* is the key to a rich flavor. Accentuate with chili bean paste adjusting the amount to your taste. Any mushroom or vegetable can be used as long as it is light in taste.

When frying eggplant, be sure to heat the pan hot enough, then add oil.
This way the eggplants will not become greasy even if more oil is used.

Spread stuffing over fried eggplant rounds. Red and yellow pepper give pleasant color combination.

Top with remaining eggplant rounds.

YU-AN STYLE SPANISH MACKEREL

Yu-an refers to a *yuzu* citron based marinade for fish or meat to be grilled.
It has been a very popular dish on the restaurant menu.

Ingredients: 4 servings

4 Spanish mackerel fillets

Yu-an marinade

- 3 tablespoons soy sauce
- 3 tablespoons rice wine
- 3 tablespoons *mirin*
- 4 slices *yuzu* citron

Sudachi or lemon citron

4 ginkgo nuts, toasted and shelled,
   optional

Pine needles, optional

Method

While marinating, turn the fillets over so they absorb the flavor from both sides.

Be sure to preheat the griddle so the fish will not stick. Brush on the marinade frequently to keep the fish soft and moist.

Marinate spanish mackerel

❶ In a shallow container blend marinade ingredients.
❷ Cut scores on the skin side of fish so it absorbs the flavor, and marinate 20-30 minutes (A).

Grill spanish mackerel

❸ Preheat a grill or griddle well. Place drained Spanish mackerel and grill both sides, brushing on the marinade several times until glazed (B).
❹ Transfer onto a serving plate and garnish with ginkgo nuts skewered with pine needles. Serve with *sudachi* citron or lemmon slices to sprinkle over fish.

Professional Hints

Mirin will cause foods to char if grilled over high heat. When both surfaces turn brown, lower the heat to cook the center.

CLAM SURPRISE

**Tasty clams are coated with egg yolk and
mushrooms, and sautéed in butter.**

Ingredients: 4 servings

20 fresh horse-neck clams in shell	6 egg yolks
1/4 onion	Salt and pepper
1 *shiitake* mushroom	Flour for dusting
2 button mushrooms	1 tablespoon butter
2-3 stalks scallion	Radish greens

Method

Preparation

❶Shell clams (A). Save shells for later use.

❷Mince onion and mushrooms. Slice scallion thinly.

❸In a bowl combine vegetables and egg yolks, and
season with salt and pepper.

❹Dust clams with flour and add to the yolk batter (B).

Sauté

❺Melt butter in a frying pan and sauté dressed clams.
Turn over and cook until golden (C).

❻Fill the empty shells with clams and arrange on a
serving platter. Garnish with radish greens and
scallion.

A

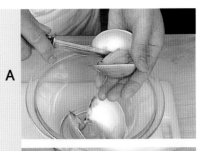

Twist open the
shells and take
out clam flesh.

B

Dress clams with
the yolk based
batter.

★
C

Sauté clams in
butter, turning
over when golden
brown. Do not
overcook, to avoid
the clams from
becoming rubbery.

BROAD BEANS AND *KONNYAKU*

**A light and healthy dish with
appetizing colors.**

Ingredients: 4 servings

200g(7 oz) shelled broad beans
   Pinch salt
1 cake(200g/7 oz) white *konnyaku*
2 tablespoon rice wine
1 boiled bamboo shoot
1/4 red bell pepper
1/4 yellow bell pepper
Cooking sauce
1 chicken bouillon cube
1 cup (200ml) water
50ml rice wine
2 teaspoons soy sauce
1 teaspoon sugar
1 tablespoon oyster sauce
Salt and pepper
Sesame oil
1 tablespoon cornstarch, dissolved in
   1 tablesppon water.

Method

Cook broad beans

❶Remove the tiny sprouts of shelled broad beans (A), and cook in boiling salted water. Drain and let stand to cool. Peel off the skin.

Cook *konnyaku* in rice wine

❷Cut white *konnyaku* into paper-thin slices and parboil; drain. In a pot put rice wine and *konnyaku*. Cook stirring until the liquid is evaporated (B).

Prepare vegetables

❸Slice bamboo shoot thinly. Parboil and blanch in cold water.
❹Seed bell peppers and cut into rolling wedges. Parboil and drain.

Cook in sauce

❺In a frying pan bring cooking sauce ingredients to a boil. Add all vegetables and *konnyaku*, and cook stirring until the flavor is absorbed. Stir in dissolved cornstarch to thicken the sauce.

★ A

By removing the tiny sprouts from broad beans, they will stay soft and fluffy when boiled.

B

Konnyaku is cooked in rice wine to give a pleasant fragrance.

Professional Hints

Since no oil is used but the cooking sauce based on chicken bouillon, this dish stays light and healthy, and at the same time you will avoid scorching the food. Enjoy variations combining vegetables of your choice.

BAKED STUFFED ONION

Onion au gratin with flavorful seafood stuffing.

Ingredients: 4 servings

4 midium size onions

6 shrimp

40g(1 2/5oz) calamari

40g(1 2/5 oz) shelled clams

60g(2 oz) broccoli, parboiled

20g(2/3 oz) canned whole kernel corn

1 cup canned white sauce

Salt and pepper

30g(1oz) butter

Parmesan cheese

Parsley

Method

Preparation

❶Trim away top and bottom ends of onions to prevent tipping. Spoon out inside to form a deep case(A).

❷Mince spooned-out onion.

❸Shell and devein shrimp, and cut in half. Make a crisscross score on calamari and cut into bite-size pieces.

❹In a frying pan melt butter and fry minced onion until transparent. Add shrimp, calamari and clam, and stir-fry. Season with salt and pepper.

❺Cut broccoli into segments and boil in salted water.

Bake and serve

❻Place seafood in onion shells and fill with white sauce, leaving the space for vegetables (B). Place broccoli and corn on top and sprinkle with Parmesan cheese. Bake in a preheated 200℃ (400℉) oven 15 to 20 minutes. Serve garnished with parsley.

A

Spoon out onions carefully so as not to damage the shape.

B

Fill onion cases with cooked stuffing and white sauce. Sprinkle with Parmesan cheese and bake until the surface becomes crisp.

Professional Hints

Shrimp, calamari and clams will get rubbery when overcooked. Be sure to stir-fry them only briefly. Since the stuffing is precooked, a toaster oven will do just as well as a conventional one.

TOFU MEUNIÈRE

Curry flavored *tofu* is fried and dressed up with colorful vegetables. A well balanced menu in every way.

Ingredients: 4 servings

1 cake soft *tofu*, drained

50g(1 3/4 oz) thinly sliced beef

Dash rice wine

1/2 package *shimeji* mushrooms

1/4 onion, thinly sliced

2-3 stalks asparagus

1/2 tomato

50g(1 3/4 oz) *udo* or celery

Watercress

Flour for dusting

Salt and pepper

30g(1 oz) butter

2 tablespoon vegetable oil

1 tablespoon milk

Sauce

2 tablespoons mayonnaise

2 tablespoons ketchup

2 teaspoons Worcester sauce

1/2 boiled egg, minced

Method

Preparation

❶Cut *tofu* horizontally in half. Cut each into 4, 8 in all. Sprinkle with salt and pepper; set aside.

❷Cut beef into bite-size pieces and sprinkle with rice wine(A). Trim *shimeji* mushrooms and cut into segments. Cut up green asparagus and parboil in salted water. Blanch and peel tomato, and cut into cubes. Shred *udo* and soak in water to remove harshness (B).

Fry *tofu*

❸Blend flour and curry powder, and coat drained *tofu* (C). Melt butter in a frying pan and fry *tofu*, turning over when browned (D-E).

❹In the same pan, heat vegetable oil and sauté beef. Add onion and cook until soft. Add mushrooms, tomato, asparagus and keep stirring(F). Add milk and season with salt and pepper.

Arrange

❺On a serving plate place drained *tofu*. Place cooked beef and vegetables on top of *tofu*. Combine sauce ingredients (G) and drizzle over *tofu*. Garnish with *udo* and watercress.

Professional Hints

Curry and butter flavors give an accent to plain *tofu*. Adjust the curry powder to your taste. Use any other garnish you wish.

A

Dash of rice wine sprinkled over beef will enhance the flavor.

B

Shred *udo* and soak in cold water until crisp.

C

Blend curry powder and flour in a shallow dish. Dust tofu pieces with the mixture.

D

Melt butter and fry *tofu*, turning when golden. Use a turner to retain the shapes.

★ E

Fry all sides until golden and transfer onto a serving dish.

F

Cook beef first, then add onion. When the onion becomes soft, add mushrooms, tomato and asparagus.

G
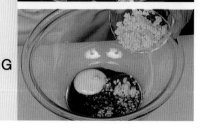
In a bowl combine mayonnaise, ketchup and Worcester sauce. Boiled egg will give a milder flavor.

ROLLED OMELETTE

**Soft and fluffy Japanese omelette is
loved for its wonderful *dashi* flavor.**

Ingredients: 4 servings

6 eggs

5 tablespoons *dashi* stock(see page 96)

To season *dashi*

1/2 teaspoon sugar

1 1/2 teaspoon soy sauce

1/3 teaspoon salt

1 tablespoon vegetable oil

5 tablespoons grated *daikon* radish

1 tablespoon soy sauce

Pinch salt

Method

Preparation

❶Season cooled *dashi* stock with sugar, light soy sauce and salt.

❷In a bowl, break eggs and mix with a fork so as not to make bubbles. Pour in *dashi* mixture and combine well; filter through a strainer (A).

Fry

❸Heat a rectangular or square frying pan till hot. Rub the surface of pan well with a cotton swab moistened with vegetable oil. Pour egg mixture in a ladle and tilt the pan so the mixture spreads evenly. When half-cooked, fold a third of the omelette toward you, then fold again to make three layers (B).

❹Wipe the bottom of pan with the oiled swab, and push the omelette away from you. Oil the near end of pan, and pour in a ladle of egg mixture. Fold again starting from the far end in the same manner (C). Repeat pouring and rolling until all egg mixture is used.

Arrange

❺Cut into thick slices and arrange them on each serving plate. Mix grated *daikon* radish with soy sauce and salt, and place in a heap as a condiment.

Professional Hints

For a smooth finish, tilt the pan so the egg mixture spreads to a thin and even layer.

★A

For a smooth texture, filter through a strainer.

★B

When pouring egg mixture, lift the egg roll slightly and let the mixture spread underneath the roll so you can roll again easily.

C

Roll quickly using chopsticks or a turner lest the heavy roll should break.

SCALLOP AND *NATTO* OMELETTE

An unexpected savoriness comes from *natto*, one of the most popular foods in Japan. Serve with the tomato sauce.

Ingredients: 4 servings

5 eggs, beaten	1 tablespoon butter
2 tablespoons milk	**Tomato sauce**
Salt and pepper	⌐ 1 large ripe tomato
1 package *natto*	1/3 onion
(fermented soybeans)	1 clove garlic
20ml soy sauce	2 tablespoons olive oil
8 fresh scallops	2 thin slices bacon
Salt and pepper	Lemon juice
1 tablespoon butter	⌐ Salt and pepper
3 *shiitake* mushrooms	1 sprig parsley
1 bunch trefoil *(mitsuba)*	

Method

Prepare eggs and sauce

❶In a bowl, mix eggs, milk, salt and pepper.
❷Mince garlic, onion and bacon. Cut up tomato.

Prepare filling

❸Mix *natto* with soy sauce, set aside.
❹Cut scallops into quarters and season with salt and pepper. Remove the stems of *shiitake* mushrooms and cut in half. Cut trefoil into 3cm (1 1/4") lengths.
❺Melt 1 tablespoon butter in a frying pan and sauté scallops over high heat (A). Add *shiitake* mushrooms and cook briefly till only the surfaces of scallops are cooked. Set aside to cool, then combine with *natto* and trefoil.

Cook omelette

❻Melt 1 tablespoon butter in a frying pan. Pour in about 90ml egg mixture and fry until the bottom is cooked and the top is still runny. Add *natto* mixture and fold up the sides of omelette. Check the shape (B).

Make tomato sauce

❼Heat olive oil in a frying pan and stir-fry garlic and bacon on low heat until the aroma is released. Add onion and keep stirring.
❽Add tomato(C), and cook until thickened to two-thirds in quantity. Season with salt, pepper and lemon juice.
❾Slide omelette onto a serving plate. Drizzle over tomato sauce, and garnish with parsley.

A

Do not overcook scallops, or they will harden.

★
B

When the bottom of egg omelette can be released from the pan, gently add filling and roll carefully so as not to damage the omelette.

C

Use ripe tomato, fresh or canned. This tomato sauce can be cooked ahead.

Professional Hints

Ten seconds can make the difference between a perfect omelette and one that is overdone. Cook quickly so the inside stays soft and fluffy.

STUFFED CHICKEN WING *TERIYAKI*

**A fun variation of gyoza. Chicken wingtips are stuffed
with shrimp paste and cooked in *teriyaki* sauce.**

Ingredients: 4 servings

12 chicken wing tips

8 prawns

50g(1 3/4 oz) Chinese cabbage

30g(1 oz) garlic chives

1 small piece ginger, grated

1 clove garlic, grated

To season filling

Salt and pepper

Dash rice wine

1 tablespoon sugar

1 tablespoon vegetable oil

Cooking sauce

4 tablespoons soy sauce

4 tablespoons rice wine

3 tablespoons sugar

Cabbage

Parsley

Method

Prepare chicken wingtips

❶Trim away tapered tips from chicken wings. Remove bones.

Prepare filling

❷Shell and devein prawns. Cut up prawns finely. Mince Chinese cabbage and garlic chives. In a bowl, combine minced prawns, vegetables, ginger and garlic. Add seasonings and "knead" well.

❸Fill chicken wings with prawn mixture and fasten with toothpicks (A).

Fry

❹Heat vegetable oil in a frying pan and fry stuffed wingtips until golden (B). Add cooking sauce ingredients and cook stirring until the liquid is thickened (C). Arrange on a serving plate and garnish with cabbage and parsley.

Professional Hints

Be sure to squeeze out moisture from minced vegetables to avoid watery gyoza. Fry jaozi over high heat until the surfaces turn golden, then reduce heat to cook the inside.

A

Stuff deboned wings and secure ends with a toothpick.

★
B

Fry stuffed wings until both sides are golden brown.

C

Add cooking sauce, reduce heat, and cook until the chicken pieces are glazed, stirring constantly.

SKILLET CRUNCHY POTATOES

Shredded potatoes and onions are fried crisp with a Japanese flavor. This is a good companion for wines or can be enjoyed as a light and healthy snack.

Ingredients: 4 servings

200g(7oz) potatoes

1/2 onion (about 50g,1 3/4 oz)

1 stalk scallion(80g,2 4/5 oz)

10g(1/3 oz) Dried *sakuraebi* (small shrimp)

Batter

- 100ml water
- 2 tablespoons dried bonito powder
- 2 egg yolks
- 6 tablespoons flour
- 3 tablespoons cornstarch

1 tablespoon vegetable oil

Basting sauce

- 2 tablespoons soy sauce
- Dash ginger juice
- Dash red hot pepper

Method

Preparation

❶Peel and shred potatoes using a mandolin (A). Soak in water and set aside.

❷Shred onion. Cut scallion into 3cm(1") lengths.

❸In a bowl combine batter ingredients and add drained potato shreds, onion, scallion and *sakuraebi* (B).

Fry

❹Heat vegetable oil in a frying pan. Place a fried-egg ring or cookie cutter on the bottom of pan and fill with potato mixture. Shape and cook until crisp, remove rings and turn to fry the other side. Baste the top with soy sauce mixture.

Professional Hints

If a right ring is not in hand, use a short, empty tin, both ends removed. Use various cookie cutter shapes, depending on the occasion.

A

Finely shred potatoes using a mandolin and blanch in water to rinse away the starch from the surfaces.

B

Use the green part of scallion or green onion. Mix well with *sakuraebi*.

★ C

Shape the mixture using a ring and fry. Remove the ring and fry the other side.

TEMPURA

A simple yet classic way of cooking which brings out the most of each ingredient. Here's how to get it right like a professional cook.

Method

Preparation

❶Make 3-4 slits on the belly side of each prawn (A) and pull ends against each other so the prawn stays straight. To prevent oil splattering, trim off the sharp ends of tails and push out moisture.
❷Slice sweet potato and pumpkin into 5mm(1/8") thicknesses. Blanch in water. Peel lotus root and cut notches to form a flower when sliced. Cut into 5mm(1/8") slices. Make a decorative criss-cross notch onto each cap of mushrooms.

Make batter and dipping sauce

❸In a measuring cup, put egg yolk and water to measure 200ml. Pour into a small bowl and mix lightly. Add flour and blend only lightly (B).
❹In a small saucepan, bring dipping sauce ingredients to a boil; allow to cool.

Deep-fry

❺Heat oil and test the temperature by dripping in a little batter. If it sinks halfway to the bottom of pot and quickly floats up to the surface of oil, it is ready. Dip ingredients in the batter and slide into the hot oil in order: prawns, smeltwhiting,

and then vegetables. It is advisable to dust seafood with flour before dipping into the batter so the batter clings well. Deep-fry for a few minutes until golden brown, turning once.
❻Arrange on individual serving plates lined with paper. Make a mound of grated *daikon* radish and ginger, and serve piping hot with the dipping sauce.

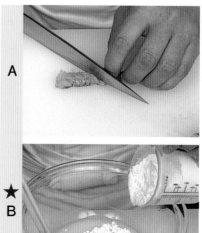

A

★

B

The slits made on the prawns will not only prevent curling but also shorten the cooking time.

For batter, use ice-cold water and do not "stir" but combine lightly, flour lumps still floating. Deep-fry a few pieces at a time for a crisp and light *tempura*.

Ingredients: 4 servings

4 prawns, shelled and deveined

2 smelt-whiting, filleted

150g(5 oz) sweet potato

150g(5 oz) pumpkin

10g(5 oz) lotus root

4 *shiitake* mushrooms

4 okra pods

Batter

⌐ 1 egg yolk

 Ice water

⌐ 1 cup(200ml) plain flour

Dipping sauce

⌐ 1 1/2 cup(300ml) *dashi* stock

 2 tablespoons light soy sauce

 2 tablespoons soy sauce

⌐ 4 tablespoons *mirin*

Vegetable oil for deep-frying

3cm(1") thick *daikon* radish, grated

Thumb-size ginger, grated

STUFFED BAMBOO SHOOT

An irresistible combination of textures, the crunchiness of lotus root and the succulent stuffing made of minced chicken and prawns.

Ingredients: 4 servings

1 small boiled bamboo shoot

80g(2 4/5 oz) minced chicken

4 prawns, heads removed

2 *shiitake* mushrooms

1 egg yolk

Batter

- 1 cup(200ml) plain flour
- 150ml water
- 1 egg yolk

Flour for dusting

Vegetable oil for deep-frying

Dipping sauce

- 300ml *dashi* stock
- 2 tablespoons light soy sauce
- 2 tablespoons soy sauce
- 4 tablespoons *mirin*
- 1 tablespoon rice wine

Condiments

Pinch salt

Pinch green tea powder

Daikon radish, grated

Ginger, grated

Lemon wedges

Method

Preparation

❶Slice bamboo shoot lengthwise into 5mm(1/8") thicknesses.

❷Shell and devein prawns, cut up until smooth, then add minced chicken, *shiitake* mushrooms, and egg yolk. "Knead" well (A) and season with salt.

Deep-fry

❸Dust bamboo shoot slices with flour and sandwich prawn mixture between them (B).

❹Combine batter ingredients, dip the sandwiches in it, and deep-fry in 180℃(360°F) oil until crisp and golden.

Serve with dipping sauce

❺Bring dipping sauce ingredients to a boil.

❻Pour the sauce into individual dishes. Mix salt and green tea powder, and put in individual dishes. Serve accompanied with a lemon wedge and a mound of grated *daikon* and ginger.

A

Mix chicken, prawns, mushrooms, and egg yolk until sticky.

★
B

Dust bamboo shoot slices with flour so the stuffing sticks. Sandwich stuffing and reshape any bulging parts.

Professional Hints

Use lightly tasted ingredients such as prawn and chicken to enhance the subtle flavor of bamboo shoot.

Ingredients: 4 servings

1 medium mackerel, filleted
 Dash rice wine
 Pinch salt
 Flour for dusting
 Breadcrumbs
2 eggs, beaten
Vegetable oil for deep-frying
40g(1 1/3 oz) onion
30g(1 oz) celery
10g(1/3 oz) carrot
Few slices ginger
30g(1 oz) dried ear mushrooms
1/2 cake soft *tofu*
100g(3 1/2 oz) minced chicken
1 tablespoon vegetable oil
30g(1 oz) green onion
2-3 stalks scallion

Cooking sauce

⌐ 1 1/2 cups *dashi* stock
 1 tablespoon soy sauce
 1 tablespoon light soy sauce
 1/2 tablespoon *mirin*
 1 teaspoon sugar
 Dash red hot pepper
 └ Dash sesame oil
1 tablespoon cornstarch, dissolved in
 1 tablespoon water

FRIED MACKEREL WITH THICK *TOFU* SAUCE

Savory thick sauce is made of vegetables and t*ofu* to enhance the rich flavor of mackerel. This dish goes well with wine or rice.

Method

Deep-fry mackerel

❶Cut mackerel into bite-size pieces. Sprinkle with rice wine and salt; set aside about 10 minutes.
❷Coat each piece with flour, beaten eggs, and bread crumbs. Deep-fry in 180℃(360℉) oil until golden brown (A).

Make thick sauce

❸Mince onion, carrot, celery, and ginger. Boil ear mushrooms and shred.
❹Cut *tofu* into 1cm(3/8") cubes. Slice green onion thinly.
❺Heat vegetable oil in a frying pan, and cook minced chicken until the color turns whitish. Add cooking sauce ingredients and cut-up vegetables except green onion, and bring to a boil. Add *tofu* and green onion (B), then thicken the sauce with dissolved cornstarch.

Serve

❻Place fried fish in a serving dish and drizzle thick *tofu* sauce over them. Sprinkle with 3cm(1") cut scallion.

38

Professional Hints

Rice wine sprinkled over mackerel upgrades the flavor. This thick *tofu* sauce can be poured over other fried fish or meat.

A

When deep-frying fish, keep the oil temperature high so the outside is light and crisp.

B

Drain *tofu* before adding it so as to avoid making the thick sauce runny.

ASPARAGUS ROLLED WITH PORK RIB

Our favorite appetizer of all time, featuring a combination of curry and cheese.

Ingredients: 4 servings

8 stalks green asparagus	Vegetable oil for deep-frying
200g(7 oz) pork rib, thinly sliced	**Coating**
Salt and pepper	┌ Dash curry powder
Flour for dusting	│ Dash Parmesan cheese
Batter	└ Pinch salt
┌ 1/2 cup(100ml) plain flour	2 tomatoes, sliced
└ 1/2 cup water	1 small cucumbers, sliced
	2 lemons, sliced

Method

Prepare asparagus

❶Discard the hard root ends. Peel one third length from ends (A).

Roll and deep-fry

❶Sprinkle pork slices with salt and pepper. Spread each slice and roll asparagus (B). Dust rolls with flour, and dip in the batter to coat evenly. Deep-fry in 180℃(360°F) oil until golden; drain oil.

Arrange

❶Mix curry powder, Parmesan cheese and salt adjusting each amount to suit your taste. Cut asparagus into bite-size pieces and dust with curry powder mix to season.

❶Arrange on a serving plate and garnish with sliced vegetables.

Professional Hints

Sprinkle curry powder mix while the rolls are hot so the flavor blends. Pork rib slices can be replaced with bacon strips.

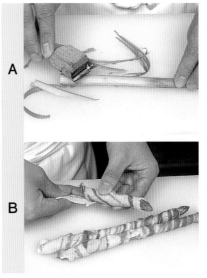

A

B

Peel the hard skin from the root ends of aspragus.

Wraps each asparagus spear tightly with a pork slice, from the root end toward the tip in a spiral.

HORSE MACKEREL ESCABOUCHE

Since it was introduced by Portuguese traders 400 years ago, this dish has been a favorite among Japanese. Here, a variety of vegetables makes the dish even lighter and tastier.

Ingredients: 4 servings

2 horse mackerel(about 600g,1 1/2 lb)
 Cornstarch for dusting
 Vegetable oil for deep-frying
50g(1 3/4 oz) *daikon* radish
50g(1 3/4 oz) carrot
1/2 red onion
1/2 each green, red, yellow pepper
1 green onion
1 pod dried red hot pepper
Marinade
- 500ml *dashi* stock
 150ml rice vinegar
 1/2 cup (100ml) light soy sauce
 70ml *mirin*
 Dash rice wine
 Dash sugar
- Pinch salt
1/2 package *daikon* radish sprouts

Method

Soak vegetables in salty water. This way they will easily absorb the marinade flavor.

Remove extra fat of deep-fried horse mackerel by pouring boiling water over it or by boiling briefly in a pot.

Marinate fish pieces with the vegetables at least 2 hours.

Preparation
❶Cut each body of horse mackerel into fillets, and remove bones along the back bone and belly. Cut into bite-size pieces and sprinkle with salt. Dust with cornstarch and deep-fry until done.

Prepare vegetables
❷Shred *daikon* radish and carrot. Thinly slice red onion and bell peppers. Place all cut vegetable in 2% salty water until supple, about 15 minutes (A).
❸Grill green onion until the outside is browned. Cut into 2cm(3/4") lengths.

Marinate
❹Bring marinade ingredients to a boil in a saucepan; set aside to cool.
❺Blanch horse mackerel in boiling water to remove extra fat (B). Add drained vegetables and dried chili pepper to the marinade. Marinate fish about 2 hours in the refrigerator (C).
❻Arrange on a serving plate and garnish with *daikon* radish sprouts, root ends trimmed off.

CHINESE SPICY PRAWNS KANDAGAWA STYLE

One of the most popular Sichuan dishes made Japanese-style with vegetables.

Ingredients: 4 servings

20 prawns

Batter

- Salt and pepper
- 1 egg white
- 3 tablespoons cornstarch

Vegetable oil for deep-frying

1/2 boiled bamboo shoot

5-6 stalks green asparagus

1/8 stalk *udo* or celery

1/3 stalk green onion, minced

Thumb size ginger, minced

1 clove garlic, minced

1 tablespoon vegetable oil

Cooking sauce

- 1/2 cup(100ml) chicken stock
- 4 tablespoons ketchup
- 2 tablespoons rice wine
- 2 teaspoons soy sauce
- 1 tablespoon sugar
- 1 teaspoon rice vinegar
- 1/2 tablespoon sesame oil

1/2 tablespoon cornstarch

Chervil

Method

Preparation

❶Shell and devein prawns. Combine batter ingredients, add prawns and mix to coat (A). Deep-fry in hot oil (B).

❷Briefly boil bamboo shoot and slice into bite-sizes. Boil asparagus in salted(not mentioned above) water. Peel *udo* and cut into julienne strips.

Stir-fry

❸Heat vegetable oil in a frying pan and stir-fry green onion, ginger and garlic until the flavors are released. Stir in prawns and bamboo shoot, then the cooking sauce ingredients (C), and bring to a boil.

Serve

❹Stir in cornstarch dissolved with same amount of water, to thicken the sauce. Add green asparagus.

❺Transfer onto a serving dish and sprinkle with *udo* and chervil.

★
A

Mix batter ingredients and coat the prawns by rubbing with fingers.

B

Deep-fry prawns in 180℃(360℉) oil until golden brown; drain oil.

C

Stir in prawns and bamboo shoot and cook briefly. Pour in cooking sauce (ketchup mixture) from the sides of the pan. Cook and stir until the sauce thickens.

41

Seasonal Menu

Spring

Although most of the vegetables appear in the grocery stores regardless of the season, a few items such as fresh bamboo shoot, fresh mountain vegetables and rape seed flower are in the market only for a short time in spring. Here is a menu to welcome spring with fresh and colorful ingredients.

SPRINGTIME *CHIRASHI-ZUSHI*

CRUMBLED EGG & *TOFU*

KONNYAKU WITH *MENTAIKO* SAUCE

SPRINGTIME *CHIRASHI-ZUSHI*

Fun to look at, fun to eat *sushi* mixed with a variety of seafood and mountain vegetables that herald spring.

Ingredients: 4 servings

3 cups(2 2/5 American cups) short grain rice	8 tablespoons sugar
300g(10 1/2 oz) minced chicken	Dash ginger juice
10 prawns, deveined	***Sushi* vinegar**
300g(10 1/2 oz) short-neck clams	70ml rice vinegar
3 dried *shiitake* mushrooms	40g(1 2/5 oz) sugar
100g(7 oz) boiled bamboo shoot	10g(1/3 oz) salt
100g(7 oz) *konnyaku*	1 tablespoon *mirin*
100g(7 oz) flowering fern (*zenmai*)	1 3cm(1 2/5") square *kombu* kelp
3 eggs, lightly beaten	1/2 lemon, squeezed
Vegetable oil for greasing	100g (7 oz) bracken
Cooking sauce	100g (7 oz) rape flowers
1/2 cup(100ml) *shiitake* soaking water	100g (7 oz) lotus root
	Some *ikura* (salted salmon roe)
1/2 cup(100ml) rice wine	Some *kinome*(young *sansho* sprout)
1/2 cup(100ml) soy sauce	Some sesame seeds

Method

Preparation

❶Rinse rice with water and steam in a rice cooker, with slightly less water than the regular rice. Boil prawns and clams and shell; set aside to cool.

❷Soak *shiitake* mushrooms in a small saucepan of lukewarm water about 30 minutes; heat briefly to accelerate softening. Cut into squares. Save the soaking water for later.

❸Cut bamboo shoot, *konnyaku* into cubes, and flowering fern, all into the same size as *shiitake*.

❹Cook bracken, rape flower and lotus root in salted(not mentioned above) boiling water; drain and cut up.

❺Make thin omelettes. Grease a heated frying pan and pour beaten eggs as thinly as possible. When the edges settle, transfer onto cutting board. Grease the pan again and repeat. When omelettes are cooled, shred finely.

Braise

❻Heat oil in frying pan. Stir-fry minced chicken, mushrooms, bamboo shoot, *konnyaku,* and flowering fern. When half cooked, add cooking sauce ingredients. Cook until most of the sauce is absorbed (A).

Make *sushi* rice

❼In a sauce pan, put *sushi* vinegar ingredients except lemon juice. Heat just until the sugar dissolves; remove from heat. Spread cooked rice in a *sushi* tub or wide and shallow dish and pour over *sushi* vinegar. Using a rice paddle, toss rice quickly (B).   When cooled, sprinkle with lemon juice (C).

Mix

❽Add minced chicken mixture and toss evenly (D). Transfer to a serving dish.

❾Sprinkle with sesame seeds, and top with prawns, short-neck clams, boiled vegetables, *ikura* and *kinome*.

Professional Hints

To enhance the flavors of seafood, add lemon juice to the *sushi* rice.

★
A

The ingredients to be mixed with rice are braised to help them hold the seasonings well.

★
B

Cooked rice is spread in a wide and shallow container while hot, and tossed quickly with *sushi* vinegar in a slicing or fluffing motion.

C

Sprinkle with lemon juice as a final touch so as not to lose the fragrance and tartness.

D

Toss rice with braised ingredients to mix evenly. Save ingredients such as prawns and clams for topping to individually taste .

CRUMBLED EGG AND *TOFU*

Easy yet deliciously seasoned *tofu* crumble featuring plentiful ingredients such as seafood and vegetables.

1 cake soft *tofu*	100g(7 oz) boiled bamboo
5 eggs, beaten	shoot
3 tablespoons sugar	⎧ 1 small can (100g /7 oz)
1 tablespoon rice wine	scallops
1 tablespoon soy sauce	100g(7 oz) green peas
1/2 teaspoon salt	⎩ Pinch of salt
5 shrimp, shelled and deveined	3 tablespoons vegetable oil
3 *shiitake* mushrooms	1 tablespoons sesame oil

Method

Preparation

❶Wrap *tofu* with a cloth to retain shape, and put a weight on it. (Use a plate or cutting board as a weight.) When extra moisture is removed (after 30 minutes), crumble with your fingers.

❷Mix eggs with sugar, rice wine, soy sauce and salt.

❸Boil shrimp and cut up. Mince *shiitake* mushrooms. Cut bamboo shoot into cubes and boil briefly. Drain scallops and separate into narrow pieces. Boil greens in salted water. Put all in the egg mixture, add *tofu* and mix well.

Braise

❹Heat vegetable and sesame oils in a frying pan. Add *tofu* mixture and cook, stirring constantly.

❺When *tofu* and eggs are cooked and crumbled, remove from heat (A) and arrange in individual dishes.

When *tofu* crumbles have almost no moisture around them, it is done.

KONNYAKU SALAD WITH *MENTAIKO* SAUCE

Light and healthy dish with an accent of chili pepper.

400g(14 oz) *ito-konnyaku*	Dash vinegar
(see page 102)	1/2 sack *mentaiko*
8 prawns, deveined	⎧ 1/2 teaspoon rice wine
50g(1 2/5 oz) green beans	1/2 teaspoon soy sauce
Pinch salt	1/2 teaspoon *mirin*
50g(1 2/5 oz) carrot	⎩ 2 radishes
50g(1 2/5 oz) mountain	*Daikon* radish sprouts
yam *(nagaimo)*	

Method

Preparation

❶Cook *ito-konnyaku* in boiling water and cut into bit-size lengths.

❷Boil prawns, shell and cut in half.

❸Cut green beans in half, and boil in salted water. Cut carrot into julienne strips and boil. Peel mountain yam and cut into julienne strips; soak in vinegared water to remove harshness and stickiness.

Toss

❹Using a blunt edge of knife, scrape *mentaiko* cod roe out of sack. Place in a bowl and mix with rice wine, soy sauce and *mirin* to make into a paste.

❺Add prepared vegetables and prawns to the bowl and toss well.

❻Arrange in individual serving dishes and garnish with thinly sliced radishes and *daikon* radish sprouts.

Adjust the seasonings according to the spiciness and saltiness of *mentaiko*. Pat ingredients dry before tossing with the sauce.

Summer Seasonal Menu

When the weather is hot and humid, nothing tastes better than the smooth touch of ice-cold *somen* noodles. Here, shrimp and vegetables are added for a balanced dinner. A spicy *aemono* salad and stir-fried dish are teamed to further stimulate your poor appetite.

DELUXE *SOMEN* NOODLES
TOMATO AND BEEF
SPICY OCTOPUS SALAD

DELUXE *SOMEN* NOODLES

Although *somen* is usually served for lunch, this version can be served as dinner.

6-8 bunches *somen* noodles (fine wheat noodles)	1 cucumber
Dipping sauce A	4 okura pods
20g(2/3 oz) dried calamari(*surume*)	20 shrimp, shelled and deveined
500ml water	Pinch salt
1 large dried *shiitake* mushrooms	4 *shiitake* mushrooms
5cm(2") square *kombu* kelp	Flowering baby cucumbers, optional
20g(2/3 oz) dried shrimp	Dash grated ginger
Dipping sauce B	2-3 stalks scallion
150m soy sauce	
150ml *mirin*	
20ml *tamari* soy sauce	
1 tablespoon rice wine	
20g(4/5 oz) dried bonito shavings	

Method

Prepare dipping sauce

❶Grill *surume* for a few seconds, and shred (A). Place in a saucepan and add remaining ingredients of dipping sauce A. Let stand about 30 minutes (B).
❷Heat the saucepan to a boil, add ingredients of dipping sauce B (C). Reduce heat and simmer about 5 minutes; set aside to cool. Filter through cheesecloth or paper towel (D).

Prepare toppings

❸Cut lotus root into flower shapes referring to page 100, if preferred, and parboil.
❹Trim away stems of fresh *shiitake* mushrooms. Grill just until the surfaces look juicy.
❺Boil shrimp in salted water. Cut cucumber preferably into shapes using a cutter (E-F). Boil okra in salted water and cut diagonally.

Cook *somen*

❻Bring ample water to a boil and cook *somen* 1-3 minutes or as directed on the package; plunge into ice water.
❼ Slice scallions thinly. Arrange *somen* in bite-size swirls using your thumb and forefinger in a bamboo basket. Arrange toppings and decorate with flowering baby cucumbers. Serve with a cup of chilled dipping sauce accompanied with grated ginger and sliced scallion to add to the sauce.

Professional Hints

Homemade dipping sauce makes the difference. Prepare a large quantity days ahead and refrigerate or freeze for later use.

A

Use kitchen scissors to shred *surume*.

★ B

Soak *kombu* kelp, *surume*, dried shrimp in water to bring out each flavor.

C

Add dried bonito shavings, cook about 5 minutes. Do not overcook or the stock will turn bitter.

D

Cool in the pan, then filter through a cheesecloth or paper towel spread over a colander.

E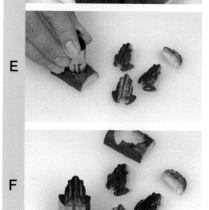

Cut vegetables such as cucumber into 1cm(3/8 ") thickness and cut out shapes using cutters.

F

TOMATO AND BEEF

Plenty of vegetables and mushrooms stir-fried
with a subtle tanginess of tomato.

Ingredients: 4 servings

4 medium tomatoes	30g(1 oz) butter
300g(10 oz) thinly sliced beef	4 tablespoons soy sauce
1 package *shimeji* mushrooms	3 tablespoons sugar
1/2 onion	Pinch salt
100g(3 1/2 oz) broccoli	Parsley, minced
100g(3 1/2 oz) cauliflower	

Method

Preparation

❶Blanch tomatoes in boiling water for a few seconds:
peel and cut up.
❷Cut beef slices into bite-size pieces.
❸Trim away root ends of *shimeji* mushrooms and cut
into segments. Slice onion in 1cm(3/8") widths.
❹Cut broccoli and cauliflower into segments. Parboil
and drain.

Stir-fry

❺Melt butter in a frying pan, sauté beef until the color
turns whitish, stir in mushrooms and onion. Then
add tomatoes (A). Season with soy sauce, sugar and
salt. When the sauce is reduced, stir in broccoli and
cauliflower.

Serve

❻Transfer onto individual serving dishes, and
sprinkle with minced parsley.

Professional Hints

The longer the tomatoes are cooked, the sweeter they
become. Adjust the time of stir-frying them according
to your taste.

A   Stir-fry tomatoes
until they lose
their shapes. If
you prefer a tangy
dish,cook briefly.

SPICY OCTOPUS SALAD

The harmony of spiciness and sweetness of kochu jang, a Korean
seasoning, is what makes this dish so appetizing. Serve chilled.

Ingredients: 4 servings

2 boiled octopus tentacles	*akadashi miso*
1 Japanese cucumber	10g(1/3 oz) white *miso*
100g(3 1/2 oz) mountain	1 tablespoon light soy
yam*(nagaimo)*	sauce
1 red bell pepper	1 tablespoon *mirin*
Dressing	1 tablespoon rice wine
⌐ 20g(2/3 oz) kochu jang	2 tablespoons honey
30g(1 oz) red *miso* (barley	Dash toasted sesame
miso)	⌐ seeds
10g(1/3 oz) *Haccho* or	2-3 stalks scallion

Method

Preparation

❶Cut octopus into bite-size pieces.
❷Make "accordion cut" on cucumber (see page 100)
and cut into 1cm(3/8") lengths..
❸Peel mountain yam and cut into julienne strips.
❹Remove stem end and seeds of bell pepper. Cut
up and parboil; drain.

Toss and serve

❺In a bowl mix dressing ingredients until well
blended. Toss octopus and vegetables (A).
❻Arrange on individual serving dish in a mound, and
top with scallion, cut into 2cm (3/4") lengths.

Professional Hints

Cucumbers absorb seasonings well and retain
crunchiness when cut accordion style. Pat dry all
ingredients before adding the dressing. Deeper flavor
will result from mixing two or more types of *miso*
paste. This blended *miso* will be good for other salads
or stir-fried dishes.

A   Toss well so that
each piece holds
the dressing.

Seasonal Menu

Autumn

Autumn provides us with the beautiful colors of changing leaves. It is also a good season for us to challenge ourselves to a new recipe using abundant, flavorful ingredients. The main course here is "Red Maple Fries" of lobster, accompanied with a simmered taro dish and creamed mushrooms.

RED MAPLE-LEAF FRIES

SIMMERED TARO AND TURNIPS

CREAMY BEEF AND MUSHROOMS

MAPLE-LEAF FRIES

The springy lobster is deep-fried and dressed with a thick sauce of colorful vegetables, resembling the autumn hues in the forest.

Ingredients: 4 servings

1 lobster	**Thick sauce**
2 Japanese eggplants (1 American eggplant)	300ml *dashi* stock
	25ml light soy sauce
5 small taro	25ml soy sauce
1/2 red bell pepper	50ml *mirin*
1/2 yellow bell pepper	Dash rice wine
50g(1 3/4 oz) snow peas, strung	Dash ginger juice
Pinch salt	1 tablespoon cornstarch
Cornstarch for dusting	1 stalk green onion, finely shredded
Vegetable oil for deep-frying	

Method

Preparation

❶Discard lobster head. Insert knife into shell and cut open to take out the flesh. Cut the flesh into bite size pieces.

❷Cut eggplants into rolling wedges. Peel small taro to form a hexagonal prism (see page 9) and slice in half.

❸Cut bell peppers into shapes using a cutter: parboil and drain. Parboil snow peas in salted water.

Deep-fry lobster and eggplants

❹Dust lobster and taro with cornstarch (A). Heat oil in a wok or fryer, and deep-fry both until golden and crisp (B).

❺Deep-fry eggplant pieces in 180℃(360℉) oil (C).

Make thick sauce

❻Bring sauce ingredients to a boil and add bell peppers and snow peas. When the surface bubbles again, stir in cornstarch, dissolved in 1 tablespoon water (D).

Serve

❼Arrange lobster, taro and eggplant in individual serving dishs, pour sauce over, and garnish with shredded green onion.

Professional Hints

Ise-ebi lobster is used here, but other lobster can be substituted for it. Other vegetables to go with the lobster are sweet potato, pumpkin and mushrooms.

A

Dust lobster pieces using a brush. Shake off extra cornstarch.

★ B

Deep-fry dusted lobster pieces until golden.

C

Eggplants do not become greasy when deep-fried in hot vegetable oil.

D

Stir in dissolved cornstarch to thicken the sauce.

SIMMERED TARO AND TURNIPS

Delicately seasoned dish using seasonal vegetables.
Enjoy the deep flavor of white *miso.*

Ingredients: 4 servings

	Cooking sauce
8 taro	5 cups(1L, 4 American
3 turnips	cups)
1/2 carrot	200g(7 oz) white *miso*
50g(3/4 oz) snow peas	20g(2/3 oz) red *miso*
Pinch salt	(barley *miso*)
1/4 *yuzu* citron, or lemon	

Method

Preparation

❶Peel taro and turnips, cut into bite-size pieces, and parboil (A). Cook taro first, and when it is half cooked, add turnips.

❷Slice carrots and cut into shapes using a cutter, and parboil. Parboil snow peas in salted water.

Simmer

❸Bring cooking sauce to a boil and add taro and turnip until the flavor is absorbed(B). When the sauce is reduced, add carrot and snow peas to cook briefly.

❹Arrange in individual dishes to form a mound and sprinkle with shredded *yuzu* citron or lemon rind.

A

Taro and turnip will retain the white color if cooked in water in which rice was rinced.

★B

Cook slowly over low heat, preferably with a dropped lid.

CREAMY BEEF AND MUSHROOMS

Mild yet rich sauce of white *miso* and sesame paste has an accent of whole grain mustard, to enhance the beef and vegetable mix.

Ingredients: 4 servings

150g(5 oz) thinly sliced beef	6 tablespoons sesame
300g/10 oz spinach	seed paste
1 package *shimeji* mushrooms	2 tablespoons white *miso*
4 *shiitake* mushrooms	2 teaspoons whole grain mustard
1 package *enokitake* mushrooms	4 tablespoons *dashi* stock
50g(1 3/4 oz) carrot	2 tablespoons soy sauce
50g (1 3/4 oz) *konnyaku*	2 tablespoons sugar
1 tablespoon vegetable oil	10cm(4") green onion
Creamy sauce	Flowering beefsteak sprigs, optional

Method

Cook beef and mushrooms

❶Cut beef and mushrooms into bite-size pieces. Heat vegetable oil in a frying pan, and stir-fry beef. Add mushrooms and cook stirring until supple. Season with salt (A).

Parboil other ingredients

❷Boil spinach; drain and cut into 3cm(1") lengths.

❸Cut carrot and *konnyaku* into julienne strips and parboil.

Mix

❹In a bowl place sauce ingredients and blend well. Add beef, mushrooms and vegetables, and mix well.

❺Transfer to individual dishes and garnish each with sliced green onion and a flowering beefsteak sprig.

★A

Stir-fry until the beef is cooked and the mushrooms become supple.

Seasonal Menu

Winter seas offer us tasty seafood including shellfish such as abalone and sea urchin. An extravagant rice recipe introduced here is very simple to cook since the ingredients taste good naturally. Fried jaozi is wrapped in *yuba*, soy milk skin. Savory Camellia Eggs look just like one of the most common blossoms in winter.

ABALONE AND SEA URCHIN RICE

FRIED JAOZI IN *YUBA*

CAMELLIA EGGS

ABALONE AND SEA URCHIN RICE

Season lightly to enjoy the natural tastes of the seafood.

Ingredients: 4 servings

1 fresh abalone (250g / 9 oz)	40ml light soy sauce
Salt	40ml rice wine
1 portion fresh sea urchin	2 tablespoons *mirin*
3 cups(2 2/5 American	└Pinch salt
cups) short grain rice	Dash *wasabi*
Cooking sauce	Chives
┌500ml *dashi* stock	

Method

Preparation

❶Separate abalone flesh from the shell and remove intestines. Cut off mouth part. Coat abalone with salt and brush away any soil, then rinse under running water (A-D).
❷Remove shell pieces from sea urchin, if any.
❸Rinse rice in a bowl and soak in water 10-15 minutes; drain in a colander.

Cook

❹In a rice cooker, place rice and abalone. Pour in cooking sauce and cook in a regular way.
❺When completely cooked, top rice with sea urchin to cook with the remaining heat.
❻Transfer onto a serving container, and sprinkle with *wasabi* and chives.

Professional Hints

Season only lightly to bring out the delicate flavor of abalone. Serve immediately after steaming fresh sea urchin on rice since it can be eaten raw and also it loses its characteristic flavor as time passes.

A To shell abalone, use a sharp wooden spatula and scrape off the flesh.

B Insert the tip of a knife between the intestine and the flesh, and trim away the ruffles and intestines.

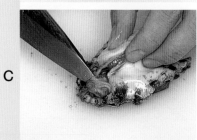

C Trim away the mouth part.

★ D Coat with ample salt, and remove any soil using a brush.

FRIED JIAOZI IN *YUBA*

**Crispy *yuba* skin holds soft, juicy
meat and shrimp filling.**
Ingredients: 4 servings

16cm (6") square *yuba* sheets (see page 104)	Dash soy sauce
100g(3 1/2 oz) minced pork	Dash sugar
70g(2 1/2 oz) shrimp	Salt and pepper
50g(1 3/4 oz) Chinese cabbage	Dash sesame oil
1/4 bunch garlic chives	1 tablespoon vegetable oil
50g(1 3/4 oz) bamboo shoot	**Dipping sauce**
Seasonings	100ml soy sauce
1 tablespoon rice wine	50ml rice vinegar
	30ml rice wine
	1 tablespoon sesame oil

Method

Cut *yuba* sheets
❶Cut *yuba* sheets into 4 squares.

Prepare filling
❷Shell and devein shrimp and mince on a chopping board. Mince Chinese cabbage and garlic chives. Cut bamboo shoot into 3mm (1/16") cubes and parboil.
❸In a bowl, mix minced pork, shrimp and vegetables, "kneading" with your hand until sticky.

Wrap and fry
❹Spread a sheet of *yuba* and wrap the filling to form a triangle.
❺Heat vegetable oil in a frying pan and fry jaozi on both sides, then the bottom (A). Blend dipping sauce ingredients; add grated *daikon* radish and red hot pepper, if preferred. Serve hot.

★ A

For crispy skin, fry over high heat, first the sides, then the bottom.

CAMELLIA EGGS

**Easy to cook savory egg dumplings will be a
conversation piece at a winter table.**
Ingredients: 4 servings

4 eggs	30g (1 oz) *ikura* (salted salmon roe)
8 quail eggs	
Dash vegetable oil	Caviar, optional
Kinome (young *sansho* sprouts)	Pinch salt

Method

Break eggs into cups
❶Spread plastic wrap and grease lightly with vegetable oil. Make 8 greased sheets. Line 8 small cups with oiled plastic wrap and break a chicken egg into 4 (A), and top with a *kinome* sprig. Break 2 quail eggs each into 4 lined cups and top with a *kinome* sprig.
❷Secure the wrap ends with elastic carefully so as not to damage the yolks. Make 8 sacks.

Boil eggs
❸Bring water to a boil in a saucepan and place wrapped eggs. Cook chicken eggs 10 minutes, quail eggs for 6 minutes (A).
❹Remove the saucepan from the heat, drain water gently so as not to damage the shapes of eggs. Let stand to cool.

Serve
❺Remove plastic wrap by scoring an "X" on the bottom, and place in serving dishes. Top with *ikura* and caviar. Serve with a salt shaker.

A

Line small cups with greased plastic wrap and place eggs into the hollows.

★ B

Cook wrapped eggs gently in boiling water.

SIMMERED DISHES & STEAMED DISHES

Nimono or simmered dishes have long been served on Japanese dinning tables to enjoy the blended flavors of the ingredients and seasonings based on *dashi* stock. Meanwhile, *mushimono* or steamed dishes are also loved as the steaming method brings out the natural flavor of food and this method of cooking is so healthy. Enjoy variations with different combinations of food and flavors.

VEGETABLE *DENGAKU*

Dengaku is *miso*-topped morsels usually skewered and grilled. This easy at-home version lets you enjoy a variety of vegetables delicately flavored with *kombu* kelp stock and dipped into the rich *dengaku miso*.

Ingredients: 4 servings

1 medium turnip	**Dengaku miso**
8 taros	100g(3 1/2 oz) *Haccho* or *akadashi miso*
200g(7 oz) lotus root	50g(1 3/4 oz) white miso
Dash vinegar	2 egg yolks
1 cake *konnyaku*	3 tablespoons rice wine
1 carrot	2 tablespoon *mirin* (see
1/2 bunch *mizuna* greens	page 102)
15cm(6") square *kombu* kelp	4 tablespoons sugar

Method

Preparation

❶Slice *konnyaku* thinly and make decorative twists (A-B).

❷Peel turnip and taro, cut into bite-size pieces, and paboil, in rice-rinsing water if possible.

❸Peel and slice lotus root, then parboil in vinegared water.

❹Cut carrots into rolling wedges and parboil(C).

❺Cut *mizuna* into 5cm(2") lengths.

Make *dengaku miso*

❻Place all ingredients in a saucepan, cook over low heat constantly stirring, about 10 minutes until glossy.

Simmer vegetables

❼Clean *kombu* kelp with a damp cloth (E). Line a pan with *kombu* and pour in hot water. Add prepared vegetables, adding *mizuna* greens lastly (F).

❽When the vegetables are cooked, serve them in the pan with *dengaku miso* dipping..

Professional Hints

This *dengaku miso* goes very well with grilled eggplant. Make a large quantity as it keeps well. Try different combinations of *miso* since each *miso* is different.

A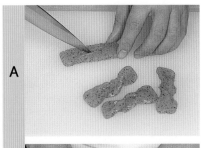

Make decorative twists with *konnyaku*. Slice *konnyaku* thinly and make a cut in the center lengthwise.

B

Pull out one end through the center slit to the other side and pull both ends.

C

Parboil vegetables and *konnyaku*. To remove harshness and retain the white color, cook turnip and taro in water used to rinse rice, if preferred.

★ D

Be sure to cook *miso* over low heat so it does not scorch at the bottom of pan. Gently stir until the mixture is glossy.

E

Clean the surface of *kombu* kelp with a damp cloth.

F

Arrange in good proportion and simmer until fork tender.

Ingredients: 4 servings

500g(1 lb) potatoes

200g(7 oz) thinly sliced beef

1 onion

2 tablespoons vegetable oil

200g(7 oz) *ito-konnyaku*

Simmering sauce

5 cups *dashi* stock

3 tablespoons sugar

2 tablespoon *mirin* (see page 102)

5 tablespoons soy sauce

100g(3 1/2 oz) snow peas

Pinch salt

Kinome (young *sansho* sprouts)

SIMMERED POTATOES AND BEEF

This is one of the most popular dishes cooked in Japanese homes. Here, the ingredients are stir-fried separately before simmering, which is the secret of this version.

Method

A

Stir-fry ingredients with a little oil to add a richer flavor.

B

Bring simmering sauce to a boil and cook stir-fried ingredients.

★

C

Reduce heat, place a drop lid or an aluminum foil on top of the ingredients, and then cover the pan to cook slowly, so the flavor of the broth is absorbed well.

Preparation

❶Peel and cut potatoes into 4 or 6. Cut beef into bite-size pieces. Slice onion. Cut *ito-konnyaku* into bite-size lengths and parboil.

❷String and parboil snow peas in salted water.

Stir-fry

❸Heat 1 tablespoon vegetable oil and stir-fry potatoes and onion.

❹In another fryong pan, heat 1 tablespoons oil and stir-fry beef and *ito-konnyaku* (A). Sprinkle with a pinch of salt.

Simmer

❺Bring simmering sauce ingredients to a boil, add potatoes, onion, beef and *ito-konnyaku*. Put a drop lid, cover and simmer on low heat about 40 minutes (C).

❻When the sauce is reduced to 1/3, add snow peas and gently shake the pan to baste all ingredients. Transfer onto a shallow dish and top with *kinome*.

Ingredients: 4 servings

2 burdock roots(about 150g-5 oz)

50g(1 3/4 oz) lotus root

30g(1 oz) carrot

70g(2 1/2 oz) *konnyaku*

1 tubular fish cake*(chikuwa)*

20g(2/3 oz) celery

3 green bell peppers

1 tablespoon vegetable oil

Simmering sauce

4 tablespoons soy sauce

4 tablespoons *mirin*(see page 102)

2 tablespoons rice wine

2 tablespoon sugar

2 teaspoons white *miso*

1/2 tablespoon sesame oil

Dash hot red pepper

Dash toasted sesame seeds

Yuzu citron rind

SPICY *KINPIRA*

Kinpira is another popular dish usually with burdock and carrot. This hot version uses seven ingredients so you can enjoy a variety of tastes and textures in one dish.

Method

Cut up ingredients

❶Cut burdock into shavings in the same manner as you sharpen a pencil(A). Peel lotus root and cut into thin half-moons; soak in water to remove harshness.

❷Cut carrot, *konnyaku*, and celery into julienne strips (B).

❸Slice fish cake thinly. Shred bell pepper.

Braise

❹Heat vegetable oil in a frying pan and stir-fry burdock, lotus root, carrot, *konnyaku* and celery until supple. Add simmering sauce (C) and cook stirring.

❺When the sauce is reduced to half, add fish cake and bell pepper. Continue cooking until the sauce has almost completely reduced.

Serve

❻Place in individual serving bowls in a mound, and garnish with sesame seeds and shredded *yuzu* citron rind. Sprinkle with red hot pepper, if preferred.

Professional Hints

White *miso* added to the simmering sauce is the key to a milder flavor.

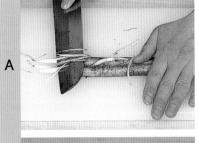
A

★ B

★ C

Make a few deep slits on burdock lengthwise, then cut into shavings as if you sharpen a pencil.

Cut vegetables except lotus root into the same size and shape. This way the heat penetrates evenly.

Blend simmering sauce ingredients ahead of time. Add to the pan when the ingredients are almost cooked. Do not overcook and retain piquant crunchiness.

SIMMERED ALFONSINO

Tasty cooking sauce brings out the best flavor of the fish.
Unexpectedly easy to cook, yet unexpectedly delicious.

Ingredients: 4 servings

4 fillets (about 500g, 2 lb) alfonsino

1/3 cake *konnyaku*

4 *shiitake* mushrooms

8 small mild green peppers

1/2 stalk green onion

Ginger, shredded

Simmering sauce

- 300ml water
- 10ml rice wine
- 4 tablespoons soy sauce
- 2 tablespoons *mirin*
- 3 tablespoons sugar

Kinome (young *sansho* sprouts)

Method

Preparation

❶Blanch alfonsino fillets in boiling water a few seconds, then plunge into ice cold water. Remove any scales and sliminess (A-B).

❷Slice *konnyaku* into thin rectagles. Make decorative twists (see page 59). Remove stems from *shiitake* mushrooms and cut decorative scores on top. Cut green onion into 5cm(2") length fine shreds, and soak in water to freshen.

Simmer

❸In a shallow saucepan, bring sauce ingredients to a boil. Add fish fillets and bring to another boil. Add mushrooms, *konnyaku*, and ginger. Place a drop lid and cook on low heat about 15 minutes until the flavor is absorbed (C).

❹Just before removing from heat, add green peppers and cook briefly.

❺Place in a serving dish and top with onion shreds and *kinome* sprigs.

Professional Hints

Fresh ginger root is a must for simmering fish. It removes the odor of fish and give it a pleasant aroma, bringing out the best of any fish. Do not layer fillets in the pan. A drop lid will allow the sauce to cover all ingredients and also prevents breaking while cooking.

A

In order to remove the fish odor and to freshen the flavor, blanch a few seconds in boiling water.

B

Plunge into cold water. Scrape off scales or soil on the skin.

★
C

Place a drop lid so the sauce will penetrate evenly. Use wooden or paper lid. Simmer over low heat.

SAKE-LEE-SIMMERED YELLOW TAIL

The distinctive flavor of *sake* lee enhances yellow tail.
Simmer with vegetables and serve as a savory soup.

Ingredients: 4 servings

800g (1 3/4 lb) yellow tail
   fillets
  Rice wine
  Pinch salt
50g (1 3/4 oz) *daikon* radish
50g (1 3/4 oz) carrot
50g (1 3/4 oz) burdock
1/2(about 50g,1 3/4 oz) *abura-*
   age (fried *tofu* pouch)
1/2 cake *konnyaku*

1 tablespoon sesame oil
Simmering sauce
  1L *dashi* stock
  100g (3 1/2 oz) *sake* lee
  60g(2 oz) white *miso*
  1/2 teaspoon salt
  1 tablespoon light soy
    sauce
Green onion, sliced
Red hot pepper

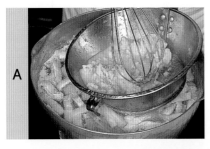

A

Dissolve *sake* lee
and *miso*
gradually in *dashi*
stock, as shown.

Method

Preparation
❶Cut yellow tail fillets into bite-size pieces. Sprinkle with salt and rice wine. Blanch in boiling water and then into cold water (see page 62).

Stir-fry
❷Cut *daikon*, carrot, *abura-age*, and *konnyaku* into thin rectangles.
❸Heat sesame oil in a frying pan, and stir-fry *daikon*, carrot, *abura-age* and *konnyaku* until they are supple.

Simmer
❹Bring sauce ingredients to a boil(A), and place fish pieces. When the fish is cooked, add stir-fried ingredients.
❺Bring to another boil and remove from heat. Serve in individual bowls, garnished with sliced green onion. Serve with red hot pepper, if you prefer.

COUNTRY CHICKEN

**Quite filling, irresistible dish
accented with bacon and garlic.**

Ingredients: 4 servings

2 chicken thighs (about 400g,14 oz)	12 button mushrooms
4 medium potatoes	Oil for deep-frying
1 medium carrot	1 tablespoon vegetable oil
12 baby onions	2 tablespoons butter
4 rashers lean bacon	3 tablespoon white wine
1 clove garlic	Salt and pepper
2 bay leaves	Parsley, chopped
	Pinch sugar

Method

Preparation

❶Cut chicken into bite-size pieces and sprinkle with salt and pepper.

❷Cut potatoes and carrots into "chateaus" with trimmed corners (A-B). Soak potatoes in water; drain and pat dry.

❸Parboil baby onions; drain.

❹Cut bacon into 1cm(3/8") squares. Slice garlic. Quarter mushrooms.

Fry potatoes

❺Deep-fry potatoes briefly in 180℃(360℉) oil.

Braise

❻Heat vegetable oil in a heavy saucepan, and sauté bacon and garlic until the aroma is released. Add chicken and sauté. Add vegetables (C) and season with salt and pepper. Add sugar, bay leaves and wine, simmer covered about 15 minutes. Add 1 tablespoon butter as a finish.

Serve

❼Melt remaining butter in a frying pan and stir-fry mushrooms. Season with salt and pepper, and add to the saucepan. Simmer a further 5 minutes. Sprinkle with chopped parsley.

Professional Hints

Sautéing chicken until browned before simmering enhances its flavor. Use cauliflower, broccoli or Brussels sprouts, if preferred.

A
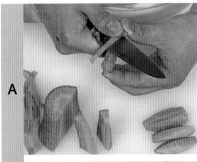

Cut carrots and potatoes into "chateaus" to prevent breakage during cooking. First cut into 5cm(2") lengths, then trim away the corners.

B

Prepared vegetables. Parboil baby onions briefly.

★
C

Sauté chicken until the surface is crisp, then add vegetables and braise.

Ingredients:4 servings

1 chicken thigh (about 200g,7 oz)

Seasonings for chicken

- 1 tablespoon rice wine
- 1/2 tablespoon light soy sauce

20cm(8") length mountain yam (*nagaimo*)

Dash vinegar

5 small sweet peppers

Cornstarch for dusting

Vegetable oil for deep-frying

Cooking sauce

- 600ml *dashi* stock
- 100ml *mirin*
- 50ml light soy sauce

BRAISED CHICKEN AND MOUNTAIN YAM

**Richly flavored dish created by deep-frying the seasoned chicken
to make an absorbent coating for the cooking sauce.**

Method

Preparation

❶Cut chicken into 8 pieces working a knife almost horizontally (see page 100).

❷Peel and slice mountain yam. Soak in vinegared water (A) for 10 minutes; drain and pat dry.

Deep-fry

❸Dust mountain yam and deep-fry in 170℃(340℉) oil until golden.

❹Pat dry chicken pieces and dust with cornstarch. Deep-fry until golden brown (B).

Simmer

❺Bring sauce ingredients to a boil, add mountain yam and chicken. Cook briefly about 3 - 4 minutes. Finally add sliced sweet peppers.

A

By soaking in vinegared water, harshness and glutenous substance are removed so the cooking sauce will penetrate easily.

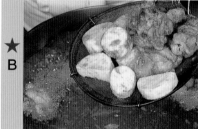

★ B

Deep-fry mountain yam. Chicken may be added to the oil to cook at a time.

Professional Hints

If the chicken is cooked in the sauce too long, the coating will come off and get soggy. The deep-frying process shortens the cooking time.

Ingredients: 4 servings

8 small taros, peeled and parboiled

1 cake soft *tofu*

Cornstarch for dusting

Vegetable oil for deep-frying

20g(2/3 oz) bean threads, softened

50g(1 3/4 oz) dried ear mushrooms

1/2 package (50g - 1 3/4 oz) *shimeji* mushrooms

1/2 red bell pepper

Simmering sauce

- 300ml *dashi* stock
- 2 tablespoons soy sauce
- 2 tablespoons oyster sauce
- 2 tablespoons *mirin*
- 2 tablespooons rice wine
- Dash grated ginger

2 teaspoons cornstarch

1 stalk green onion, shredded

Coriander

BRAISED TOFU WITH THICK VEGETABLE SAUCE

Smooth and tasty bean threads hold the vegetables together to be poured over deep-fried *tofu* and taro.

Method

Deep-fry

❶Drain *tofu* (A) and cut into 8 cubes

❷Heat oil to 180℃(360℉) in a wok or fryer. Coat *tofu* with cornstarch and deep-fry until golden. Deep-fry taro. Set aside.

Prepare vegetables

❸Cook bean threads in boiling water 2-3 minutes and plunge into cold water; cut into 5cm(2") lengths.

❹Cook ear mushrooms in boiling water and shred. Trim and separate *shimeji* mushrooms into segments. Cut up pepper and parboil.

Make sauce

❺Bring simmering sauce ingredients to a boil, and add prepared vegetables. Bring to a boil again, stir in cornstarch dissolved in 4 teaspoons water (B).

❻Place *tofu* and taro in a serving dish, drizzle thick sauce, and top with shredded onion and coriander.

Wrap *tofu* in a cloth, and put a weight on to drain out moisture. Use a heavy dish or bowl as a weight.

Since bean threads and mushrooms cook easily, finish with dissolved cornstarch when the liquid bubbles again.

Professional Hints

Oyster sauce is the key to the deep flavor of the sauce.

★ A

Clean clam shells by rubbing them between your palms.

★ B

Cook clams only briefly. 1 table-spoon of butter can be saved to give flavor at this stage.

★ C

Add remaining vegetables and stir-fry, sprinkling the seasonings over. Add curry powder finally so the flavor will not be released away.

Preparation

❶Place clams in salted water 4-5 hours in a dark place to allow them to expel sand and dirt. Rinse in clean water, rubbing between your palms to remove dirt from the shells (A).

❷Divide broccoli and cauliflower into bite-size florets and parboil in salted water.

❸Seed bell pepper and cut into strips.

Cook

❹Heat butter in a frying pan and stir-fry onion and garlic. Add clams (B), broccoli and cauliflower. When all clams open, add bell pepper and the seasonings already mixed. Cook and stir so the flavored juice will coat every piece (C).

Serve

❻Transfer onto a serving dish and sprinkle with chopped parsley.

Professional Hints

Stir-fry onion until supple so its natural sweetness is extracted. Do not overcook clams as they will become rubbery.

CURRIED CLAMS

Savory clams enhanced with rice wine and curry while the vegetables are enlivened by the delicious clam juice.

Ingredients: 4 servings

700g(1 1/2 lb) clams in shell

100g(8 oz) broccoli

100g(8 oz) cauliflower

Pinch salt

1/2 red bell pepper

1/2 onion, minced

1 clove garlic, minced

2 tablespoons butter

Seasonings

⌐ 1 teaspoon rice wine

  2 teaspoons curry powder

∟ Pinch salt

Parsley, chopped

Ingredients: 4 servings

230g(1/2 lb) pumpkin

80g(2 4/5 oz) sweet potato

80g(2 4/5 oz) minced chicken

30g (1 oz) green beans

Pinch salt

Simmering sauce

500ml *dashi* stock

2 tablespoons soy sauce

1/2 tablespoon *mirin*

1 tablespoon sugar

3 tablespooons whipping cream

Dash roasted soybean flour(*kinako*)

SNOW-TOPPED PUMPKIN AND SWEET POTATO

**Delicately sweet simmered dish with
whipped cream on top.**

Method	Professional Hints

When simmering pumpkin and sweet potato, it is recommendable to place a drop lid so the cooking sauce will cover all pieces. Since the cooking time depends on the type of pumpkin, check doneness by inserting a skewer; if it goes smoothly, it is done.

Preparation

❶Seed pumpkin, cut into bite-size pieces, and trim off corners (A).

❷Slice sweet potato into 2cm(3/4") thicknesses and soak in water.

❸Bring water to a boil in a saucepan, and blanch minced chicken in a colander to remove extra fat. Cut green beans into halves and parboil in salted water.

Simmer

❹Bring sauce ingredients to a boil and place pumpkin, sweet potato, and chicken. Cook slowly over low heat so the cooking sauce is absorbed. Just before the cooking sauce is reduced completely, add green beans.

❺Place in a serving dish in a mound, and top with whipped cream (B). Sprinkle with roasted soybean flour.

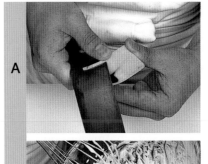

A

Cut pumpkin into bite size pieces, peel partially and round off corners so they will retain their shapes.

B

Whip cream until stiff and place on top, resembling snow.

69

ROLLED CABBAGE IN CREAM SAUCE

Chicken and shrimp stuffed cabbage rolls simmered in flavorful cream sauce give a delicate taste with a silky smooth texture.

Ingredients: 4 servings

8 cabbage leaves

Salt and pepper

200g(8 oz) minced chicken

1/2 onion

30g(1 oz) carrot

4 *shiitake* mushrooms

2 tablespoons vegetable oil

1 egg yolk

Cream sauce

- 400ml water
- 2 chicken bouillon cubes
- 100ml fresh cream
- Salt and pepper
- Dash sesame oil
- Dash oyster sauce

4 teaspoons cornstarch

1/3 red bell pepper

1/3 yellow bell pepper

Coriander leaves

Method

Prepare vegetables

❶Parboil cabbage; drain and sprinkle with salt; allow to cool.

❷Shell and devein shrimp. On a cutting board, cut up coarsely (A).

❸Mince onion. Shred carrot and *shiitake* mushrooms, stems removed.

Prepare stuffing

❹Heat 1 tablespoon oil in a frying pan, and stir-fry onion until transparent. Add carrot and mushrooms and continue cooking, allow to cool.

❺In a bowl, put minced chicken, shrimp, egg yolk, and cooked vegetables. Using your hand in a kneading motion, mix well until the mixture becomes sticky. Season to taste with salt and pepper.

❻Form one portion of stuffing into a ball, and wrap with a cabbage leaf. Secure the end with a tooth pick (B).

Sauté and simmer

❼Heat 1 tablespoon oil in frying pan, and sauté cabbage rolls until the surface is browned. Add cream sauce ingredients and simmer 12-13 minutes over medium heat. Dissolve cornstarch with double amount of water, and stir in to thicken the sauce.

❽Serve garnished with shredded peppers and coriander leaves.

A

Chop shrimp coarsely so some springy texture will remain.

★
B

Form one portion of stuffing into a ball, and wrap with boiled cabbage leaf.
Secure the end with a toothpick.

QUICK ROAST DUCK

Brown-sautéed duck meat perfectly harmonizing with the quick sauce. Together it tastes special.

Ingredients: 4 servings

400g(116 oz) top quality duck
meat(crossbreed between
mallard and Japanese duck)
150ml *tonkatsu* sauce, or Worcester
sauce plus 20g(2/3oz) sugar
80ml ketchup

100ml white wine
1 tablespoon sugar
Salt and pepper
Cherry tomatoes
Watercress

★
A

Cook the skin side
slowly until the fat
comes out, turn
over and cook
until lightly
browned.

B

Place browned
duck meat in the
sauce, and cook
slowly in an oven
or toaster oven.

Method

Brown meat

❶Trim away extra fat from the duck meat. Sprinkle with salt and pepper. Cut scores on the skin side.
❷Heat a frying pan and place duck meat skin side down, and cook until the fat seeps out. Turn and cook the other side briefly (A).

Simmer in oven

❸In a casserole or oven-proof pan, put *tonkatsu* sauce, ketchup, white wine and sugar, and bring to a boil.
❹Add the duck(B). Cover and cook in 200℃(400℉) oven about 7 minutes. Take out from the oven and allow to cool.
❺When cooled enough to touch, slice thinly and arrange on a serving plate. Garnish with cherry tomatoes and watercress. Pour remaining sauce.

Professional Hints

Duck meat has thick fat under the skin. Score deeply and finely on the skin side so the extra fat will be released when cooked, which is the key to the aromatic flavor.

SEA BREAM STEAMED WITH CLAMS

A whole sea bream is a symbol of best wishes and has been served on many celebration tables. This deluxe version uses sea vegetable and clams steamed together, to enhance the delicate flavor of the bream. Try with any white meat fish.

Ingredients: 4 servings

1 sea bream, about 1kg (2 lb)	*Ponzu* dipping sauce
Pinch salt	⎡ 200ml water
16 clams	200ml soy sauce
300g (10 oz) *wakame* seaweed	100ml rice vinegar
50g (1 3/4 oz) *daikon* radish	100ml *mirin*
50g (1 3/4 oz) carrot	1 tablespoon rice wine
100ml rice wine	⎣ 5cm(2") square *kombu* kelp
1 stalk green onion	Dried bonito shavings
10cmx20cm(4"x8") *kombu* kelp	2 *sudachi* citron, squeezed, or 1 lime
	Daikon radish, grated with red hot pepper
	Green onion, finely shredded

Method

Preparation

❶Rinse sea bream, sprinkle generously with salt; set aside about 20 minutes.

❷Place clams in salted water 4-5 hours in a dark place to allow them to expel sand and dirt. Wash in clean water, rubbing between your palms.

❸Soak *wakame* until soft, and cut into bite-size pieces.

❹Cut *daikon* and carrot into flower shapes and parboil.

Steam

❺Line a casserole with *kombu* kelp, place the sea bream. Place clams around the fish and cover with *wakame* (A). Sprinkle with rice wine and steam in a boiling steamer 20-30 minutes (B). Add parboiled vegetables to warm for the last 3 minutes.

Make *ponzu* dipping sauce

❻Heat sauce ingredients except bonito and *sudachi*, and just before the boiling point add bonito shavings (C); immediately turn off the heat and allow to cool. Filter through paper towel and mix with citron juice.

❼Finely shred the white part of green onion cut into 5cm(2") lengths. Soak in cold water to freshen.

❽On a serving plate place sea bream with clams and *wakame*. Garnish with drained onion. Serve with *ponzu* sauce mixed with grated *daikon* radish.

Professional Hints

Fillets of sea bream or other white meat fish can be used as well. Also, bottled *ponzu* is now available for busy people.

A — Lightly wipe *kombu* with a damp towel, and lay in the bottom of pan.

★B — Top with *wakame* to entirely cover the fish and clams. Sprinkle with rice wine.

C — Add dried bonito shavings as a finishing touch, to give a fine aroma to *ponzu* sauce.

SAVORY EGG CUSTARD

**The silky smooth texture and the delicate taste of
this dish will never fail to please your guests.**

A

Use *dashi* stock
cooled well. Mix
with the eggs, and
strain in a fine
sieve.

★
B

Straining the egg
mixture results in
a smooth
consistency.

C

Place the
ingredients in
each cup and
ladle in the egg
mixture gently.

Ingredients: 4 servings

3 eggs, beaten	8 shrimp
400ml *dashi* stock	4 slices wheat flour gluten (*namabu*,
2 teaspoons *mirin*	shaped like a cherry blossom)
1/2 teaspoon salt	4 small *shiitake* mushrooms
1/2 teaspoon light soy	4 ginkgo nuts
sauce	Trefoil (*mitsuba*)
100g(3 1/2 oz) chicken thigh	*Yuzu* citron rind

Professional Hints

When steaming, reduce heat about half through the cooking
time and do not overcook, to prevent rough and spongy texture.

Method

Prepare egg mixture

❶Bring *dashi* stock, *mirin*, salt and light soy sauce to
a boil; allow to cool to room temperature. Add beaten
eggs and strain the mixture through a fine sieve to
achieve a smooth consistency (A, B).

Prepare ingredients

❷Cut chicken into thin strips, and blanch in boiling
water. Devein shrimp, cook in boiling water, and
shell. Discard stems from *shiitake* mushrooms, and
cut a decorative criss-cross notch on each top. Boil
shelled ginkgo nuts and remove skin.

Steam

❸Fill a steamer with water and bring to a boil. Turn off
from heat and place individual cups.   Arrange one
portion of the ingredients in each and pour in egg
mixture gently (C).   Cover and steam 8-10 minutes.
❹Blanch trefoil in boiling water. The custard is done
if a toothpick inserted into the center comes out clean.
Garnish with trefoil and citron rind. Put the lid back
and serve hot with a spoon.

ONE-POT COOKING

Nabemono, or one-pot cooking, is served not only for the simplicity of the preparation but also for friendship. It is fun for any number of people to surround a cooking pot at the dining table. Of numerous recipes, the best ones are arranged in Kandagawa style.

SEAFOOD IN *MISO*-BUTTER POT

**Seafood that are best in winter
cooked in rich *miso* and butter sauce.**

Ingredients: 4 servings

1 lobster	1 package *shimeji* mushrooms
300g(10 oz) shelled oysters	**Broth**
Cornstarch for dusting	1200ml *dashi* stock
8 small taros	100g(3 1/2 oz) white *miso*
1 cake *tofu*	40g(1 2/5 oz) red *miso*
100g(3 1/2 oz) broccoli	20g(2/3 oz) *Haccho* or *akadashi miso*
100g(3 1/2 oz) cauliflower	2 tablespoons butter
Pinch salt	Chives

Method

Preparation

❶Cut unshelled lobster into bite-size pieces (A).

❷Coat oysters with cornstarch and rub with your fingers to clean; rinse off(C).

❸Peel and parboil taros.

❹Cut broccoli and cauliflower into florets and parboil in salted water. Trim *shimeji* mushrooms and cut into segments.

Cook at the table

❺In a shallow pot, bring broth ingredients to a boil. Add lobster pieces and cook. Add oysters, taro and *tofu*, and bring to another boil. Add broccoli, cauliflower, mushrooms and butter. Sprinkle with generous amount of chives. Set the table with individual bowls and a ladle to serve the delicious broth.

Professional Hints

Prawns or crabs can be used in place of lobster. Use any selection of vegetables, but be sure to use several kinds for a better taste.

Butter added at the last step gives a deeper and milder flavor blended with *miso*.

A

Remove legs and head from the lobster.

B

Cut unshelled lobster into bite-size pieces. Cook with the head, only to extract the flavor, not to eat.

★
C

Coat oysters with cornstarch and rinse in water. This way any dirt will be washed away from oysters.

ICEFISH AND EGG POT

**The light broth sets off the delicate taste of
Japanese icefish and vegetables.**

Ingredients: 4 servings

200g(7 oz) Japanese icefish

  Pinch salt

1 boiled bamboo shoot, about 300g(10 oz)

100g(3 1/2 oz) lily bulb

100g rape seed flower

Cooking sauce

  ┌480ml *dashi* stock

  │ 40ml light soy sauce

  │ 40ml *mirin*

  └40ml rice wine

3 eggs

Kinome (young *sansho* sprouts)

Method

Preparation

❶Rinse Japanese icefish in salted(about 3%) water; drain(A).

❷Cut bamboo shoot into thin slices, and parboil.

❸Separate lily bulb into cloves. Cut rape seed floweer in half. Parboil both.

Simmer

❹In a shallow earthenware pot, bring sauce ingredients to a boil. Add bamboo shoot and icefish (B). Bring to another boil and add lily cloves and rape flower. Beat eggs and drizzle in a swirling motion (C). When half set, remove from heat and sprinkle with *kinome* sprouts.

Professional Hints

Do not overcook icefish. Also, remove from the heat when the eggs are half set. The pot will do the rest of cooking for a soft, fluffy texture. Season only lightly so as not to spoil the delicate flavor of the fish, lily bulb, and bamboo shoot.

★A Rinse icefish in salted water. This way the fish will be cleaned without losing its flavor.

B Cook bamboo shoot and icefish only briefly so they will not become tough.

★C Drizzle in beaten eggs through a perforated spoon in a swirl. Do not cook until completely set.

76

COUNTRY *SUKIYAKI*

This is a simple version of the popular beef dish cooked at the table, adding delicious vegetables that are full of dietary fiber.

Ingredients: 4 servings

800g(1 3/4 lbs) beef sirloin, very thinly sliced

1 medium onion

1 burdock

100 g rape seed flower

1 bunch (50 g) fiddlehead fern *(warabi)*

1 bunch (50 g) flowering fern *(zenmai)*

1 boiled bamboo shoot (about 300g-10 oz)

4 eggs

1 package *kinome* (young *sansho* sprouts)

Cooking sauce

150ml *dashi* stock

150ml rice wine

150ml soy sauce

150ml *mirin*

2 1/2 tablespoons sugar

Dash *sansho* pepper, optional

A

Use lots of mountain vegetables including burdock which is the best companion of beef. Cut each into similar sizes.

Method

Preparation

❶Cut beef slices into bite-size pieces. Half the onion and slice into 1cm(3/8") thicknesses.

❷Cut burdock into shavings(see page 100) and soak in water to remove harshness. Parboil rapeflower and ferns, plunge into cold water and set aside; drain and cut into 5cm(2") lengths. (A)

Cook at the table

❸Set a portable gas stove on the dining table and put a shallow pan on it (or use an electric skillet). Pour in cooking sauce and cook beef. Add vegetables and continue cooking.

❹Set each place with an individual serving bowl. Break one egg into each so the diner mixes with chopsticks and dip the cooked ingredients into it before eating. Sprinkle with *kinome* and *sansho* pepper, if preferred.

RICES/NOODLES/SOUPS

Popular everyday meals introduced here vary from a simple one-bowl rice or noodle dish with favorite toppings to a "variety" rice cooked with lots of ingredients and savory broth.

VARIETY RICE

**Enjoy the natural flavor of each ingredient
cooked with rice and broth.**

Ingredients: 4 servings

3 cups(2 2/5 American cups) short grain rice

150g(5 oz) chicken thigh

60g(2 oz) burdock

60g(2 oz) carrot

1 sheet *abura-age*

1/2 cake *konnyaku*

3 dried *shiitake* mushrooms, softened

50g(1 3/4 oz) snow peas, strung

1 tablespoon vegetable oil

Pinch salt

Seasonings for stir-frying

- 1 teaspoon soy sauce
- 1 teaspoon rice wine
- 1/2 teaspoon *mirin*
- Pinch salt

Cooking broth

- 500ml *dashi* stock
- 40ml soy sauce
- 40ml rice wine
- 2 tablespoons *mirin*
- Pinch salt

Method

Preparation

❶Rinse rice in water and drain in a colander; let stand at least 30 minutes (A).

❷Dice chicken. Cut burdock into thin shavings (see page 100), and soak in water to remove harshness. Shred carrot finely.

❸Remove extra oil from *abura-age* by scalding or blanching in boiling water (B). Parboil *konnyaku* and cut into 3cm(1") long shreds. Cut *shiitake* mushrooms into the same size.

Fry and steam

❹Heat vegetable oil in a frying pan and stir-fry chicken and prepared vegetables. Add seasonings (C).

❺In a rice cooker, place rice, cooking broth, and stir-fried ingredients. Steam in the same manner as the regular rice.

❻Boil snow peas in salted water; drain. Let the rice steam after the switch is turned off, about 10 minutes. Place in individual serving bowls and garnish with shredded snow peas.

Professional Hints

Shred ingredients as finely as possible so they hold the seasonings well. The key is stir-frying the ingredients before cooking with the rice.

A

Drain washed rice for about 30 minutes.

B

Remove extra oil from *abura-age* by blanching into boiling water. This way *abura-age* will hold the flavors well.

★ C

Cook and season ingredients before steaming with rice.

ZOSUI KANDAGAWA STYLE

Zosui is a rice gruel cooked with a little rice for easy digestion and usually served hot. This is a summmer version to encourage your poor appetite. Use left-over rice.

Ingredients: 4 servings

3 cups(2 2/5 American cups) cooked rice

4 shrimp

Dash rice wine

100 mountain yam*(nagaimo)*

1/2 bunch trefoil *(mitsuba)*

2 pickled Japanese plums

Cooking broth

- 4 cups(3 1/5 American cups) *dashi* stock
- 1 tablespoon light soy sauce
- 1 teaspoon salt
- Dash rice wine

Remove starch from the cooked rice by rinsing under running water.
Immediately drain in a colander so as not to prevent sogginess.

Bring the broth to a boil and cook rice and shrimp. Both should not be cooked too much.

Cool in ice water at once since the rice will absorb all the moisture as time goes.

Method

Preparation

❶Rinse cooked rice under running water to remove starch (A) and drain in a colander.

❷Shell and devein shrimp. Cut into 1cm (3/8") lengths. In a small saucepan, place shrimp and sprinkle with rice wine. Cook stirring until the moisture evaporates.

❸Peel mountain yam and cut into tiny cubes. Parboil trefoil and cut into 2cm(3/4"). Remove stones from pickled plums and chop with knife for a smooth texture.

Cook in broth

❹Bring the broth ingredients to a boil (B) and add rice and shrimp. Bring to another boil; remove from heat and dip the pan in ice water to cool (C).

❺When completely cooled, transfer into individual serving bowls and top with mountain yam, trefoil and pickled plum.

Professional Hints

Since cooked rice absorbs moisture quickly, do not overcook. Try with other ingredients such as greens and mushrooms. Serve hot in cooler seasons.

TEA AND RICE WITH EEL

This simple fare started as an end to the meal, pouring green tea over the remaining rice in your bowl and eating with some pickled vegetable. This rich version uses delicious eel simmered with *sansho* pepper.

Ingredients: 4 servings

2 *teriyaki*-broiled eel	⌐1 tablespoon *tamari* soy sauce
1 tablespoon Arima *sansho* peppercorn	⌐1 tablespoon sugar
Cooking sauce	4 cups cooked rice
⌐200ml rice wine	Green tea
100ml soy sauce	Rice cracker bits, optional
100ml *mirin*	Pickles, optional

Method

Prepare eel

❶Cut broiled eel into 1.5cm(1/2") squares (A).
❷Bring cooking sauce ingredients to a boil, and cook eel in it over low heat (B). When the sauce is reduced to half, add Arima *sansho* and continue cooking until the liquid is almost reduced (C).

Serve

❸Place 1 cup cooked rice in individual bowls, top with several pieces of eel. Pour over hot green tea and serve immediately, accompanied with rice cracker bits and pickles of your choice.

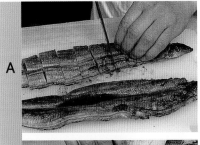
A

Cut broiled eels into bite-sized pieces.

B

Bring the cooking sauce to a boil, reduce heat and add eel to simmer.

★ C

Add *Arima sansho* when the liquid is reduced to half, and keep simmering.

Professional Hints

Arima is the place name of a suburb of Kobe, known for its production of *sansho*. Arima *sansho* represents preserved corn simmered in soy sauce and other seasonings. It is soft and has a piquant and deep flavor, which enhances various dishes as well as plain white rice. Any dish whose name begins with Arima means it has the *sansho* fragrance.

CHESTNUT RICE

This is a traditional autumn dish in Japan, providing the subtle sweetness of lightly seasoned ripe chestnuts.

Ingredients: 4 servings

2 2/5 cups(2 American cups) short grain rice	**Cooking sauce**
1/3 cup(1/4 American cup) glutenous rice	600ml *kombu* stock
	2 tablespoons rice wine
	1 teaspoon salt
500g(1 lb) fresh chestnuts	1 teaspoon light soy sauce
1/2 package edible chrysanthemum flower	1/2 bunch trefoil *(mitsuba)*
	Toasted sesame seeds

Method

Prepare chestnuts

❶Place unshelled chestnuts in a large bowl. Bring water to a boil and allow to cool to 60-70℃(140-160℉). Pour this water on chestnuts and let stand 20-30 minutes until the shell is soft.

❷Drain chestnuts in a colander. Using a paring knife, cut off the hard bottom, then peel the shell in a pulling-up motion. Pare the inner skin in the same manner. Cut chestnuts into 2 or 3 pieces, and soak in water to remove bitterness.

❸Chestnuts need a further step to remove bitterness. Bring ample water to a boil, add chestnuts and bring to another boil. Continue heating over high heat 2-3 minutes; drain and soak in water 4-5 minutes.

Steam rice

❹Wash and drain two kinds of rice. Place in a rice cooker and pour in cooking broth. Add chestnuts and set the cooker as usual. Let steam 10 minutes after it turns off.

❺Separate chrysanthemum flowers into petals and center; discard the centers. Parboil petals, and plunge into cold water; soak while cooking rice. Parboil trefoil and cut into 1cm(3/8") lengths.

❻Place cooked rice in a serving dish, and sprinkle with trefoil, chrysanthemum petals, and sesame seeds (A-B).

Professional Hints

Carefully skin the chestnuts as any remaining inner skin will spoil the taste and the color when cooked. Cook them over high heat so the bitterness will be removed and the color stays bright.

Drain chrysanthemum petals and squeeze out moisture before sprinkling over the rice.

Sprinkle with trefoil and sesame seeds attractively. The toppings work as an accent to the simple rice.

RICE-STUFFED CALAMARI

This dish is a Western version of the popular *ika-meshi*, or kalamari rice. Savory butter rice is stuffed in kalamari and steamed in white wine. Serve with the tomato sauce.

Ingredients: 4 servings

Rice stuffing

- 1 cup(1 1/5 American cups) short grain rice
- 1 tablespoon minced onion
- 1 tablespoon butter
- 1 chicken bouillon cube
- 300ml boiling water

2 kalamari

1 green bell pepper

1/4 red bell pepper

2 tablespoons minced onion

1 tablespoon minced garlic

3 tablespoons vegetable oil

Salt and pepper

70ml white wine

2 tablespoons tomato purée

4 tablespoons ketchup

Parsley sprigs

Method

Prepare rice

❶Wash and drain rice. Melt butter in a heavy frying pan, and fry minced onion until transparent. Add rice and cook until almost transparent.

❷Dissolve bouillon cube in the boiling water and add to the pan. Transfer into a rice cooker and steam in the usual way; let steam 10 minutes after the switch turns off.

Prepare calamari and vegetable

❸Clean and trim the calamari to make 2 tubes. Remove skin and pat dry.

❹Cut bell peppers into 5-6mm(about 1/8") squares.

Make stuffing

❺Heat 1 tablespoon vegetable oil and stir-fry bell peppers. Season with salt and pepper.

❻Add the cooked rice (A) and stir-fry with minced parsley (save some sprigs as a garnish).

❼Stuff calamari with the rice (B) and secure the ends with toothpicks.

Steam

❽Place the stuffed calamari in a saucepan, add wine. Cook over high heat, then reduce to low to simmer.

❾In the frying pan heat vegetable oil and sauté garlic and onion. Add tomato purée and ketchup, and season with salt and pepper.

❿Slice calamari into 2cm(3/8") widths and arrange on a serving plate with the sauce. Garnish with parsley.

★A

Stir-fry bell peppers, add cooked rice and mix in minced parsley.

B

Stuff the calamari with cooked rice pressing to pack tightly.

Ingredients: 4 servings

Pork cutlets

4 80g(2 4/5 oz)pork loin cutlets

- Salt and pepper
- Flour for dusting
- 2 eggs, beaten
- Breadcrumbs
- Oil for frying
- 1/2 onion

1/2 bunch trefoil (*mitsuba*)

4 eggs, beaten

Cooking sauce

- 200ml *dashi* stock
- 50ml soy sauce
- 50ml *mirin*
- 1 tablespoon sugar
- 1 tablespoon rice wine

4 portions cooked short grain rice

PORK CUTLET ON RICE

Popular one-bowl dish. Enjoy the contrast of crisply fried cutlet and the fluffy omelette in savory sauce.

Method

Prepare pork cutlet

❶Make a few scores against the border line of the meat and the fat, to prevent curling. Sprinkle with salt and pepper. Coat with flour, eggs, then breadcrumbs, and deep-fry in hot oil; drain and keep hot.

Cook in sauce

❷Slice onion thinly. Cut trefoil into 3cm(1") lengths.

❸In a saucepan bring cooking sauce ingredients to a boil. Add onion and bring to a simmer. Add trefoil and cook only 10 seconds. Pour in beaten eggs in a swirl. Cook just until the eggs begin to set, without stirring; remove from heat (A).

❹Place one portion of rice in a large bowl, place sliced pork cutlet, and top with the omelette. Pour remaining sauce over to seep down (B).

A

Pour in beaten eggs gently and evenly. Cook until the edges set without stirring.

B

Place cutlet and top with the fluffy omelette, while hot.

Professional Hints

This version cooks the pork cutlet and the eggs separately so that the coating of the cutlet will remain crisp. If you prefer juicy coating, lay the sliced cutlet in the cooking sauce and pour it over the cutlet to cook together with the eggs.

Preparation

❶Peel mountain yam and grate finely. Cut trefoil into 3cm(1") lengths.

❷Mix grated mountain yam, flaked salmon, pickled red ginger, egg and trefoil in a bowl (A) and divide into quarters.

Fry

❸Heat vegetable oil in a frying pan and pour in one portion of egg mixture. Cook both sides, turning once (B).

Make thick sauce

❹In a small saucepan bring *dashi* stock, soy sauce and *mirin* to a boil. Dissolve cornstarch in double amount of water and stir into the sauce to thicken.

❺Place one portion of rice in individual serving bowls, and cover with the omelette. Pour on thick sauce (C) and garnish with *wasabi* and *nori*.

Professional Hints

Stop cooking when the egg mixture becomes fluffy and lightly browned.

A

Mix mountain yam, salmon and other vegetables well.

★ B

Pour egg mixture into frying pan. Cook until the bottom is lightly browned; turn and cook the other side alike.

C

Drizzle the glossy thick sauce over the omelette for the finished dish.

EGG FOO-YONG ON RICE

Quick and easy one-bowl dish using canned salmon and mountain yam. *Wasabi* horseradish and the shredded *nori* give an accent to the soft and mild flavor.

Ingredients: 4 servings

200g(7oz) mountain yam*(nagaimo)*

30g(1 oz) bottled flaked salmon

4 eggs

10g(1/3 oz) pickled red ginger*(beni-shoga)*

1/2 bunch trefoil *(mitsuba)*

1 tablespoon vegetable oil

Thick sauce

┌200ml *dashi* stock

│40ml soy sauce

│20ml *mirin*

└2 teaspoons cornstarch

4 portions cooked short grain rice

Dab of *wasabi*

Nori seaweed, shredded

COLD NOODLES WITH SPICY MEAT SAUCE

Rich and spicy Chinese meat sauce goes surprisingly well with the smooth and plain cold noodles.

Ingredients: 4 servings

200g(7 oz) dried Japanese noodles *(udon)*

200g(7 oz) minced beef and pork

3 tablespoons rice wine

1 clove garlic, minced

1 thumb size knob ginger, minced

1 eggplant

1/2 red bell pepper

Vegetable oil for deep-frying

1 tablespoon sesame oil

1/2 bunch green onion

Cooking sauce

- 400ml water
- 2 chicken bouillon cubes
- 2 tablespoons *Haccho* or *akadashi miso*
- 2 tablespoons sugar
- 1 teaspoon chili bean paste

2 teaspoons cornstarch, dissolved in same amout of water.

Method

Cook noodles

❶Cook noodles as directed on the package. Plunge into cold water, immerse quickly and drain in a colander.

Prepare sauce

❷Sprinkle minced meat with rice wine and mix (A).
❸Cut eggplant and bell pepper into rolling wedges (see page 100). Deep-fry in hot oil; drain.

Cook sauce

❹Heat sesame oil in a frying pan and sauté garlic and ginger until the aroma is released. Add minced meat and stir-fry until the color turns whitish. Combine cooking sauce ingredients and add to the pan. Cook for a further 2-3 minutes. Add deep-fried eggplants and pepper. Stir in dissolved cornstarch to thicken.
❺Arrange noodles attractively on a serving plate, and add meat sauce next to them or pour over. Garnish with shredded green onion.

Professional Hints

Deep-frying gives the eggplant and pepper a richer flavor to go with the meat. When cooking the sauce, keep stirring so it does not scorch at the bottom of pan. This meat sauce is a good companion to boiled vegetables as well.

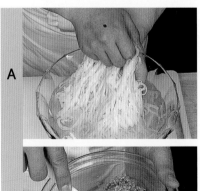

A

When the noodles are cooked, drain and plunge into ice water to tighten the consistency.

B

Sprinkle rice wine over the minced meat to bring out the flavor.

MEATBALLS ON GREEN NOODLES

**Delicious chicken balls top the hot cooked noodles
in delicately flavored soup.**

Method

Prepare meatballs

❶In a bowl place minced chicken and the seasonings. Mix well until sticky using your hand to "knead" (A).

Prepare vegetables

❷Trim *shiitake* mushrooms and cut in half. Slice carrot and cut into flower or maple leaf shapes, using a cutter. Parboil carrot.

Cook noodles

❸Bring ample water to a boil and cook noodles as directed on the package; drain in a colander.

Finish and serve

❹Bring soup ingredients to a boil, and drop one scoop of the minced chicken, using a spoon to form a ball (B).
❺When the balls float to the surface, add vegetables and cook briefly.
❻In individual serving bowls, place noodles and the toppings. Pour in soup.

A

★
B

Blend the seasonings well with the minced chicken until sticky with your hand. Add sliced green onion.

Bring soup ingredients to a boil. Forming the seasoned meat into a round shape, drop each into the soup to cook.

Professional Hints

Mountain yam makes the meatballs mild in taste and smooth in texture. Be sure to mix vigorously to bring out the glutenous consistency of the yam. Also, a dash of ginger juice plays an important role.

Ingredients: 4 servings

150g(5 oz) minced chicken

Seasonings for chicken

- 2 tablespoons grated mountain yam
- 1 egg yolk
- 1 tablespoon sliced green onion
- 1 teaspoon *Haccho* or *akadashi miso*
- 1 teaspoon sesame paste
- 1/2 teaspoon soy sauce
- 1/2 teaspoon *mirin*
- Pinch salt
- Dash ginger juice

2 *shiitake* mushrooms

1/3 medium carrot

Green onion, diagonally sliced

Soup for noodles

- 1600ml *dashi* stock
- 100ml light soy sauce
- 50ml *mirin*
- Pinch salt
- 1 teaspoon rice wine

4 bunches dried green buckwheat noodles*(chasoba)*

Ingredients: 4 servings

300g(10 oz) fresh white asparagus

2 tablespoons milk

30g(1 oz) leek

30g(1 oz) onion

30g(1 oz) potato

1 tablespoon butter

300ml boiling water

90ml fresh cream

Salt and pepper

1/2 tomato, diced

2-3 stalks scallion

CREAM OF ASPARAGUS SOUP

**The spring delicacy is made into a
creamy soup.**

Method

Prparation

❶Cook asparagus in salted water with a dash of milk(not mentioned above) until soft (A). Trim away tough skin at the root ends, and cut up. Save the tips for garnish.

❷Place asparagus and milk in a blender or food processor, and liquefy. Strain through a sieve and chill.

Cook potato

❸Slice onion and leek. Peel and slice potato thinly and rinse in water.

❹Melt butter in a saucepan, cook onion and leek slowly until soft. Add potato slices and cook until transparent over low heat (B).

❺Dissolve bouillon cubes in boiling water and add to the pan. Cover and cook until the potato becomes soft. Liquefy again in a blender or food processor; strain and chill.

Serve

❻Combine asparagus purée and stock. Add fresh cream, salt and pepper. Serve chilled.

★
A

Add some milk to the water to cook asparagus whitish.

★
B

Fry onion and leek slowly over low heat to bring out the sweetness.

88

Method	Professional Hints

Preparation

❶Shell broad beans. Tear the top of skin a little, and cook in salted water. Drain and allow to cool. Skin, and save 12 beans for garnish.

Cook beans

❷Slice onion and leek thinly. Melt butter in a saucepan and fry them slowly over low heat. Add broad beans (A) and fry. Dissolve bouillon cube in hot water and add to the pan. Cover and simmer about 10 minutes. Finally add spinach to cook only briefly to retain color.

Blend in a blender

❸Place the cooked vegetables with stock in a blender. Liquefy and strain through a sieve (B).

❹Put back to the saucepan and cook over low heat with fresh cream and milk. Season to taste with salt and pepper.

❺Serve garnished with boiled broad beans, croutons and watercress.

To bring out the fresh green color, boil the broad beans in heavily salted water. Also, do not let the onion and leek turn brown while frying. This method can be adapted to other bean, pea or pumpkin soup.

A

★
B

Add broad beans and fry slowly over low heat. Pour in broth and simmer.

Strain through a sieve to obtain a smooth texture. Take time to strain the thick mixture.

CREAMY BROAD BEAN SOUP

**This nutritiously well-balanced soup captures
the flavors of spring in its fragrance and color.**

Ingredients: 4 servings

500g(1 lb) broad beans

30g(1 oz) onion

30g(1 oz) leek

1 chicken bouillon cube

300ml hot water

6 spinach leaves

45ml fresh cream

180ml milk

1 tablespoon butter

Salt and pepper

Garnish

  Croutons

  Watercress

GYOZA SOUP

Splendid combination of popular Chinese dim sum and a tangy vegetable soup for "greedy" palates

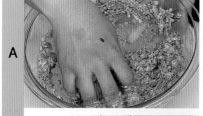

A Mix stuffing ingredients in a "kneading" motion until the consistency becomes sticky, to blend the flavors.

B Scoop one portion of stuffing with a spoon or spatula, and wrap with the skin. By moistening the edges of skin you can seal securely.

★ C Cook onion and only the white parts of bok choy first as they are tougher.

D When they are supple, add bok choy leaves and tomatoes.

E When the soup comes to a boil, add jiaozi and cook.

F Constantly skim off foam while cooking.

G Finally add stir-fried vegetables to cook only briefly.

Ingredients: 4 servings

100g(3 1/2 oz) minced pork	1/2 onion
70g(2 1/2 oz) shrimp	1 bok choy
50g(1 3/4 oz) Chinese cabbage	2 tomatoes
	1 tablespoon sesame oil
1/4 bunch garlic chives (*nira*)	**Soup stock**
50g(1 3/4 oz) bamboo shoot	┌ 1 L water
20 jiaozi skins	2 chicken bouillon cubes
Seasonings for stuffing	1 tablespoon soy sauce
┌ 1/2 teaspoon soy sauce	1 tablespoon rice wine
1/2 teaspoon sugar	Dash ginger juice
1/2 teaspoon sesame oil	└ Salt and pepper
1 tablespoon rice wine	
└ Salt and pepper	

Method

Prepare stuffing

❶Mince Chinese cabbage and garlic chives and sprinkle with salt; let stand 10 minutes and squeeze out moisture. Shell and devein shrimp and cut up finely. Cut bamboo shoot into 5mm(1/8") cubes.
❷In a bowl, place minced pork, vegetables and seasonings, and mix well until sticky using your hand (A).

Wrap and boil

❸Wrap the stuffing in jiaoizi skins (B) and cook in boiling water 2 minutes; drain and set aside.

Make soup

❹Cut onion and bok choy into julienne strips. Cut tomatoes into 2cm (3/4") cubes.
❺Heat sesame oil in a frying pan, and stir-fry onion and the white parts of bok choy (C). When they become supple, add tomatoes and green leaves of bok choy (D).
❻Bring soup stock ingredients to a boil, and cook jiaozi (E). Skim off any foam (F), and add stir-fried vegetables (G). Bring to a boil and immediately remove from heat and serve.

Professional Hints

It is essential to squeeze out as much moisture as possible for the best result. Use any selection of vegetables for the soup.

OYSTER AND BACON SOUP

The simplest recipes are often the most delicious. This is not an exception, with the rich flavors of oyster and bacon, cooked with ample vegetables.

Ingredients: 4 servings

300g(10 oz) shelled oysters

1 tablespoon cornstarch

3 Chinese cabbage leaves

200 rashers bacon

50g(1 3/4 oz) carrot

3 *shiitake* mushrooms

1 stalk green onion

1/2 bunch trefoil *(mitsuba)*

Soup stock

1L chicken stock

1 teaspoon light soy sauce

1/2 teaspoon salt

Dash ginger juice

Dash sesame oil

3 teaspoons cornstarch

2 eggs

Method

Preparation

❶Coat oysters with cornstarch. Wash off any dirt or shell particle together with the cornstarch coating (A-B). Pat dry and dust with cornstarch again. Blanch in boiling water and plunge into ice water to tighten the flesh (C).

❷Cut Chinese cabbage and bacon into bite-size pieces. Shred carrot. Remove stems of mushrooms and slice thinly.

❸Slice green onion thinly. Cut trefoil into 3-4cm(1"-1 1/2").

Cook

❹Bring soup stock ingredients to a boil, add oysters and vegetables. When it comes to a boil, stir in cornstarch dissolved in double amount of water, to thicken. Finally add trefoil, then stir in beaten eggs to "bind".

Professional Hints

Oysters need a little preparation to get the most of the delicate flavor. Also do not overcook them as they become tough. Try with other vegetables of your choice.

★A

Cornstarch coating makes the cleaning easy.

★B

After rubbing with the cornstarch, wash off in clean water.

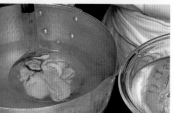

★C

The second coating will prevent oysters from shrinking. Blanch in boiling water, then plunge into ice water to tighten the flesh.

CLEAR SOUP OSAKA STYLE

Traditional clear soup featuring
okonomi-yaki, an Osaka's specialty.

Ingredients: 4 servings

50g(1 3/4 oz) cabbage, shredded

50g(1 3/4 oz) lean pork, thinly sliced

2 shrimp, shelled and deveined

2 tablespoons mountain yam *(nagaimo)*

1 egg

2 tablespoons plain flour

1 tablespoon vegetables oil

Soup stock

- 600ml *dashi* stock (see page 96)
- 40ml light soy sauce
- 40ml rice wine
- 20ml *mirin*

Shaved *kombu* kelp *(tororo)*

Green onion to garnish

Method

Preparation of *okonomi-yaki*

❶Cut up pork and shrimp.

❷In a bowl, combine shredded cabbage, pork, shrimp, grated mountain yam, egg and flour (A). Mix well and divide into 8.

❸Heat vegetable oil in a frying pan, and place one portion of the cabbage mixture in a round shape. Fry both sides (B). Make 8 *okonomi-yaki* rounds.

Make soup

❹In a saucepan, bring soup stock ingredients to a boil.

❺Place 2 *okonomi-yaki* rounds in each serving bowl, pour in soup stock (C) and garnish with shaved *kombu* and sliced green onion.

Professional Hints

Grated mountain yam *(nagaimo)* is essential for a fluffy *okonomi-yaki*. When frying, preheat the frying pan hot for crispy surfaces.

A

★
B

C

Cut the ingredients as finely as possible. Bind them with grated mountain yam and eggs.

Shape into rounds and fry until browned, turning once.

Pour in stock and serve immediately. Garnish with shaved *kombu* and green onion, if preferred.

ESSERTS

When it comes to enjoying desserts, Japanese people are no exception. Here are two light-tasting, healthy examples using less sugar.

Ingredients: 4 servings

200g(7 oz) strawberries

200g(7 oz) melon

1/2 Philippine mango

Gelatin base

500ml water

100g(3 1/2 oz) sugar

15g(1/2 oz) unflavored gelatin

1/2 lemon, squeezed

Yogurt sauce

100ml natural yogurt

Sugar

Mint sprigs to garnish

FRUIT CRYSTAL

Colorful selection of fruits are encased in clear jelly.

Method

Preparation

❶Halve or quarter hulled strawberries. Cut melon and mango into the same sized cubes.

Make jelly

❷In a saucepan put water and dissolve sugar. When the temperature reaches 60℃(140℉), remove from heat and stir in gelatin powder to dissolve; allow to cool. When it is cooled to room temperature, add lemon juice.

❸In a square mold, arrange fruit pieces. Gently pour in gelatin base and chill in the refrigerator until set, about 2 hours (A).

Serve

❹Add sugar to the plain yogurt to adjust sweetness.

❺Cut jelly into portions and place on individual serving plates. Pour on yogurt sauce and garnish with a mint sprig.

★
A

Use any selection of fruit, taking the color combination info account.

CREAMY SWEET POTATO IN POPPY SEEDS

Irresistible contrast of creamy sweet potato filling and crunchy poppy seed coating.

Ingredients: 4 servings

200g(7 oz) sweet potatoes	Pinch salt
60ml fresh cream	**Coating**
20g(2/3 oz) cream cheese	Plain flour for dusting
2 tablespoons sugar	2 egg whites
Dash brandy	100g(7 oz) poppy seeds
	Vegetable oil for deep-frying

Method

Preparation

❶Cut sweet potatoes into 3cm(1") slices, and steam in a steamer until soft.

❷Peel and strain through a sieve (A).

Shape and deep-fry

❸Mix strained sweet potatoes with fresh cream, cream cheese, brandy, sugar and salt. Shape the mixture to resemble golf balls(B).

❹Coat each ball with flour, beaten egg white, then with poppy seeds (C). Deep-fry in 170-180℃(340-360°F) oil.

A

★ B

C

Strain steamed sweet potatoes through a sieve for a smooth texture.

Blend with fresh cream, cream cheese, etc. to give even smoother texture. Shape into balls, rolling between your palms.

Coat with poppy seeds completely and deep-fry.

BASIC *DASHI* STOCK

Dashi, the essential soup stock and seasoning in Japanese cuisine, can be made in different ways according to need. Although today much Japanese home cooking depends on instant mixes called "*dashi no moto*", it is worth making the *dashi* yourself for special occasions. It is not so complicated as you may think. Make a large quantity and keep refrigerated.

Primary *Dashi* (left)

This is used for clear soups and simmered dishes that are lightly or delicately seasoned.

Secondary *Dashi* (right)

This is more widely used for miso soups, one-pot dishes, and simmered dishes that are heavily seasoned.

Primary *Dashi*

Ingredients

1 L(1 quart) water

7cm(3") square *kombu* kelp

30g(1 oz) dried bonito shavings

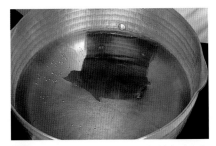

❶Fill a saucepan with 1 L water and add the *kombu* kelp. Let stand 30 minutes, and place over medium heat.

❷When the water begins to bubble just before the boiling point, take out *kombu*. Be careful since *kombu* emits a bitter flavor after the water boils.

❸Add dried bonito flakes at once. When the flakes settle at the bottom of pan, remove from heat.

❹Filter through a colander lined with cheesecloth or paper towel. Do not squeeze for primary *dashi*.

Secondary *Dashi*

Ingredients

1L(1 quart) water

Kombu kelp and bonito flakes, reserved from primary *dashi*

10g(1/3 oz) dried bonito flakes

❶Fill a saucepan with the water, reserved *kombu* and bonito flakes. Bring to a boil.

❷When the water boils, add a further 10g(1/3 oz) dried bonito flakes, and cook about 10 minutes. These additional bonito flakes are called "*oi-gatsuo*".

❸Filter through a colander lined with cheesecloth or paper towel, pressing down to squeeze out moisture.

Reserving *dashi* stock

Make a large quantity and freeze in ice cube tray or container, and store in the freezer.

Dashi Stocks for Noodles

Dipping sauce or soups for Japanese noodles are based on the following *dashi* stock. Adjust the ratio of soy sauce, *mirin*, etc., depending on the kind of noodle as indicated below(Be sure to heat *mirin* and *rice wine* to a boil so the alcohol evaporates).

①Fill a saucepan with 1L(1 quart) water and add 1 dried *shiitake* mushroom and 8cm(3") square *kombu* kelp cleaned with a damp cloth. Let stand at least 30 minutes.

② Heat to a boiling point. Add 15g(1/2 oz) dried bonito flakes and 20g(2/3 oz) dried small sardines *(niboshi)*. Cook 7-8 minutes over medium heat. Filter through a colander lined with cheesecloth or paper towel.

Dipping Sauce for *Somen*

600ml basic stock for noodles

200ml rice wine

100ml soy sauce

100ml light soy sauce

200ml *mirin*

Broth for *Udon* and *Soba*

800ml basic stock for noodles

50ml light soy sauce

25ml *mirin*

1 tablespoon rice wine

Pinch salt

Dipping Sauce for *Soba*

700ml basic stock for noodles

140ml soy sauce

4 tablespoons *tamari* soy sauce

200ml *mirin*

1 tablespoon sugar

CUTTING INTO SHAPES

It would be no exaggeration to say the success of a dish most often depends on the proper cutting of the ingredients. There are appropriate shapes for the types of vegetable and the recipes.
Use a sharpened knife and practice cutting slowly but steadily at first.

Rounds

for *daikon* radish, carrot, etc

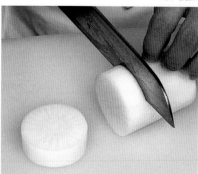

Peel and slice crosswise. The thickness depends on the recipe: 1.5-2cm(1/2"-3/4") for simmered or steamed dishes, 1-2cm(3/8"-3/4") for salads and dressed dishes.

Half-moons and quarter rounds

for *daikon* radish, carrots, etc

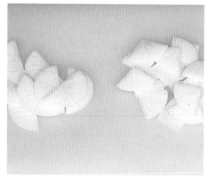

For half-moons, cut cylindrical vegetable in half lengthwise, then slice crosswise into required thickness. For quarter rounds, cut cylindrical vegetable into quarters, then slice.Slice thinly for salads, and thickly for cooked dishes.

Rectangles

for carrot, burdock, *daikon*, etc.

Cut vegetable into 5cm(2") lengths, then slice lengthwise into thin (7mm-1cm, 1/4"-3/8") even slices.

Julienne strips or matchsticks

for carrot, burdock, etc.

Cut a stack of rectangles lengthwise into thin strips. When cutting into the rectangles, check the thickness with the recipe.

Rolling wedges

for carrot, lotus root, pepper, bamboo shoot, etc.

Cut a corner of the vegetable diagonally, rotating between cuts so each piece is about the same size. Often used for simmered or stir-fried dishes.

Dices or cubes

for carrot, *daikon*, bamboo shoot, etc.

Cut vegetable lengthwise into strips of required thickness, then crosswise into cubes or dices.

Shreds

for cabbage, onion, etc.

Stack thin slices or leaves and cut into fine strips, as thinly as possible. Mainly used for salads.

Wedges

for tomato, citron, etc.

Round vegetables can be cut this way. Cut in halves lengthwise, then cut each half into three or four.

Thin slices

for green onion, *myoga*, etc.

Simply slice thinly from the edge of vegetable.

Diagonal slices

for green onion, burdock, etc

Slice diagonally crosswise, into about 1cm(3/8") widths. Mainly used for simmered or one-pot dishes (*nabemono*).

Shredding green onion

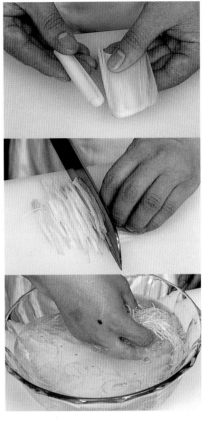

First cut into 5cm(2") lengths, then split lengthwise and remove the green core. Spread the white part and shred finely along the fibers. Soak in cold water to freshen. Used as a garnish or condiment.

Mincing onion

Split in half lengthwise. Place the cut face down, make two or three deep cuts holding the knife horizontally as shown. Shred finely along the fibers, leaving the root end uncut to hold the shreds in place. Holding the knife across the fiber, shred finely.

Shaving burdock

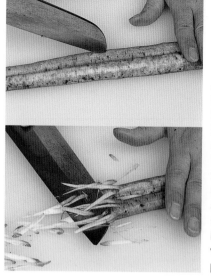

A good way to cut a very thin and tough vegetable like burdock is shaving. Make two or three slits lengthwise, then move the knife along the fiber rotating the burdock as if you were sharpening a pencil.

Horizontal slicing

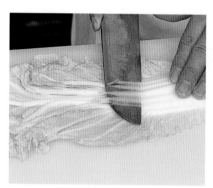

This is used for slicing thin and large vegetables. To slice the thick white part of Chinese cabbage, work a knife almost horizontally and slice, securing the vegetable with another hand. Also used for slicing *sashimi* or chicken.

Accordion cut for cucumber

for cucumber

Cut deep slits (do not cut through) diagonally across cucumber, at as narrow intervels as possible. Turn over and make the same slits diagonally. Cut into 2cm(1") lengths. This is an efficient way of cutting cucumber for salads or dressed dishes as it absorbs the seasonings well while retaining crunchiness.

Chateau cuts

for carrot, potatoes, etc.

Cut vegetable into 5cm(2") lengths, and split in two or four. Trim away the corners to make round shapes. Used as a decorative cut or as an functional trimming for simmered dishes.

Katsuramuki technique for *daikon* radish

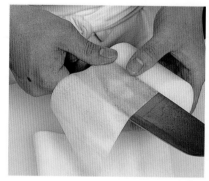

Cut radish into 5-10cm(2"-4") long cylinders, then "peel" thinly as you rotate the cylinder using the other hand. For even thickness, push away the radish with your thumbs and move the radish rather than the knife which moves subtly back and forth.

Blossom cut for lotus root

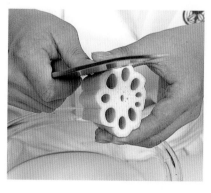

Peel off the skin. Working the knife along the holes, trim away the parts between "petals" deeply. Slice into desired thickness.

GLOSSARY OF INGREDIENTS

ABURA-AGE(DEEP-FRIED TOFU POUCH)

Abura-age is deep-fried *tofu* sliced thinly. It is fried until the outside becomes crisp and golden brown but the inside is still white.

BAMBOO SHOOT

Bamboo shoots are one of the most common ingredients in Asian cooking. In Japan, bamboo shoots are "cooked-fresh", canned in water and available all year-round. Such water-packed bamboo is exported and available in U.S.

BEAN THREADS

These are long, dry noodles made of mung bean flour. They keep on the shelf indefinitely. Soak them in warm water for 15 minutes before use. They may also be deep-fried in hot oil. (Do not soak them in water prior to deep-frying) Use them as a noodle in soups, or with stir-fried vegetables and meat. Break off amount needed and store remainder in the bag.

BEEFSTEAK PLANT(*SHISO*)

These minty, aromatic leaves come in green and red varieties. The red type is used to make *umeboshi* (pickled plum).

CHINESE CABBAGE

This versatile, greenish-white leafed cabbage is used in stir-fried and one-pot dishes. It is also added to soups, and made into pickles. A heavy, succulent vegetable, Chinese cabbage is often found in supermarkets, not to mention oriental food stores. It is also known as "celery cabbage" and "*nappa* (sometimes 'Napa') cabbage." Avoid produce

with spotted leaves, if possible. Store as you would with lettuce.

DAIKON RADISH

Daikon radish is rich in vitamins, and its leaves contain much calcium. Freshly grated radish helps digestion. It is good for simmered dishes as well.

DRIED BONITO

This is an important ingredient in *dashi* stock. A dried bonito fillet looks like a 6-8in (15-20cm) long brownish hunk of wood.

Shaved, dried bonito flakes are also available in packs and convenient to use.

Dried bonito "thread" shavings are often used as a garnish. Such "thread" shavings look like rosy-beige excelsior and have a pleasant flavor. If you cannot obtain them, use regular dried bonito flakes.

DRIED *WAKAME* SEAWEED

This seaweed is usually sold in dried or salted form, so soak in water to soften before use. *Wakame* seaweed can be used for various soups. It is also a good salad ingredient. It should not be simmered more than a minute. Rich in vitamins and proteins.

EGGPLANT

The size of eggplant varies with region and season. Japanese eggplant is smaller and softer compared to American. Substitute with half number of American eggplants.

ENOKITAKE MUSHROOM

Enokitake mushrooms are mild-flavored and have a pleasant crispness and aroma. They are often used in soups. There are canned *enokitake* mushrooms but fresh ones are better.

GINGER ROOT

Choose ginger root that is firm and tight. Avoid pieces that are flabby or have soft spots. Pare skin of amount you will use.

SMALL CUCUMBER

Recipes in this book call for small cucumbers which needs no peeling or seeding. However, to smooth the rough surface and to bring out the skin color, dredge the cucumber in salt and roll it back and forth on a cutting board using the palm of your hand. Wash well.

KAMABOKO / *CHIKUWA* (STEAMED FISH PASTE)

Kamaboko is made mainly from fish protein. Good *kamaboko* is white and elastic and the cut end is glossy. Keep in refrigerator. *Chikuwa* literally means ring of bamboo. Both *kamaboko* and *chikuwa* go well with

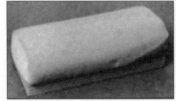 

horseradish soy sauce.

KOMBU KELP

Kombu is one of the basic ingredients used for making *dashi* stock. When you use it, never wash or rinse. The speckled surface of the kelp holds flavor, so just wipe with a damp cloth. Kelp contains the most iodine of all seaweeds.There are salted ones that are cut into squares to be eaten as a relish.

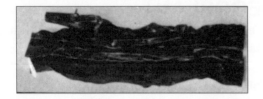

KONNYAKU / *ITO-KONNYAKU*

Konnyaku, made from a gelatinous mountain tuber has almost no calories. It needs heavy seasoning as it has a bland taste. *Ito-konnyaku* is a strip form of *konnyaku*.

 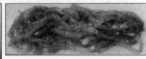

LOTUS ROOT

The flesh is white and "crunchy". Long tubular hollows run through the entire length of the root. When preparing lotus root for cooking, pare it first. Then cut into rounds. The shape should be attractive.

To prevent discoloring it should be immersed for a short time in a mixture of vinegar and water. This also gets rid of any harshness in flavor. It can then

be boiled in water containing a little vinegar. It goes well with vinegared dishes.

MENTAIKO (CHILI COD ROE)

This is fresh cod roe preserved in salt and chili. Since it was introduced from Korea where *mentaiko* means just "cod roe", it has become very popular in Japan for everyday meals. It makes great dressings for seafood or vegetable salads, and even for spaghetti.

MIRIN

Mirin is heavily sweetened *sake* or rice wine, made to be used for cooking. Rice wine or sherry sweetened with sugar can be a substitute.

MISO

Miso is fermented soybean paste. The colors range from yellow to brown; yellow *miso* is referred to as white *miso* in this book. Brown *miso* is called red *miso*. Since there are various kinds of *miso*, it might be helpful to learn about *miso* by buying small quantities of various kinds. It is used for soups, dressings, sauces, etc.

NATTO

This is a fermented soybean preparation made by the action of special bacteria. It has a rich cheese-like flavor and is sticky. With good *natto*, the sticky "threads" formed while being mixed  should be strong and stubborn and the beans should be moderately moist.

NIBOSHI

Niboshi is made from small sardines. These are soft-boned fish which are sun-dried. They are used for fish stock. The fish stock has rather a strong flavor and it is used for *miso* soup or noodle broth.

NORI SEAWEED

The best quality *nori* seaweed is glossy black-purple. It is used after toasting which improves flavor and texture. *Nori* seaweed grows around bamboo stakes placed under water. When the time comes, it is gathered, washed, laid in thin sheets and dried. it contains lots of iodine.

PICKLED PLUM (*UMEBOSHI*)

Pickled plums are made in June when green plums come onto the market in Japan. Green, unripe plums are soaked in brine, packed with red *shiso* leaves and left to mature in the vinegar bath. In Japan *umeboshi* have long been regarded as a tonic. Not only are they thought to help in digestion, but they also keep the intestinal tract clear. This may be one of the reasons why *umeboshi* are served with the traditional Japanese breakfast. Also, *umeboshi* paste is used as a dressing ingredient.

RED HOT PEPPER

Red pepper is used fresh or dried. Dried and ground coarse pepper is called *ichimi*, or one flavor spice. This *ichimi* is one of the component ingredients of *shichimi* or seven-spice mixture. *Shichimi* is a collection of seven dried and ground flavors:red pepper flakes; roughly ground, brown *sansho* pepper pods;minute flakes of dried dark green nori seaweed bits; and white sesame seeds.

RICE VINEGAR

Japanese rice vinegar is milder than most Western vinegars. Lightness and relative sweetness are characteristics of rice vinegar. Use cider vinegar rather than anything synthetic if substituting.

RICE WINE

Rice wine is made by inoculating steamed mold (*koji*) of rice and then allowing fermentation to occur. It is then refined. In Japan rice wine is the most popular beverage, but it is also used in various ways in cooking.

SAKURAEBI (SMALL SHRIMP)

Tiny shrimp that is almost transparent or in the color of cherry blossom, or *sakura*, hence the name. Usually sold in a dried form to be used as a *tempura* ingredient.

SANSHO, KINOME SPRIGS

Both the leaves and seed pods of *sansho* are used. Dried leaves are powdered and used as a spice, *sansho* pepper. The young leaves, called *kinome* sprigs, are mainly used to garnish foods.

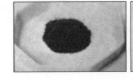 

SESAME OIL/SESAME PASTE

Made from sesame seeds which are rich in oil and protein, this oil has a unique taste and aroma. It is mixed with salad oil and used for frying *tempura* or to add flavor and aroma to the dressing for Japanese-style *aemono* dishes. Sesame paste, finely ground sesame seeds, is favored for its nutty flavor. Used for dressing and dipping sauces.

SESAME SEEDS

Both black and white sesame seeds are used in Japanese cooking. When toasted, sesame seeds have a much richer flavor. Richer still however, are ground sesame seeds. To grind sesame seeds use a *suribachi* (Japanese grinding bowl). Before grinding, toast seeds in a dry frying pan. It is a nice garnish.

SHIITAKE MUSHROOM

Both fresh and dried *shiitake* mushrooms are readily available. Dried ones should be soaked in water before using. This soaking water makes *dashi* stock (Japanese soup stock). Fresh *shiitake* mushroom has a distinctive, appealing "woody-fruity" flavor. *Shiitake* mushrooms are good for simmered dishes because of their special flavor. The best ones have thick, brown velvety caps and firm flesh.

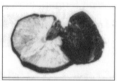

SOY SAUCE/*TAMARI* SAUCE

Soy sauce is made from soybeans and salt. It is the primary seasoning of Japanese cooking. It is used for simmering foods, dressings, soups and many kinds of Japanese dishes. Ordinary soy sauce is dark, but one which has a light color is also available. The light soy sauce does not darken the colors of food, and it is salty enough. *Tamari* is a special thick, subtly sweet soy sauce used as a dip for *sashimi*.

TOFU

Tofu, "bean curd" in English, is an important product of soybeans. It is rich in proteins, vitamins, and minerals. It is low in calories and saturated fats, and entirely free of cholesterol.

There are two types: cotton *tofu* and silk *tofu*. Cotton *tofu* is firm. Silk *tofu* is softer and contains more whey.

TREFOIL(*MITSUBA*)

Trefoil is a member of the parsley family. The flavor is

somewhere between sorrel and celery. It accents the flavor of many Japanese dishes.

UDO(ARALIA CORDATA)

For Japanese, *udo* is one of the vegetables that herald spring. Its special fragrance and crisp texture are favored in dressed dishes (*aemono*) and soups. To prevent discoloring, soak in water for about 10 minutes after slicing. *Udo* may be substituted with celery as it somewhat resembles in both texture and flavor.

WASABI

Wasabi is Japanese horseradish. It is pale green in color. It has a more delicate aroma and is milder tasting than Western horseradish. In Japan both fresh and powdered *wasabi* are available, but it is hard to obtain fresh *wasabi* in other countries. It usually comes in a powdered form or in a tube, but the fragrance of fresh *wasabi* is much richer than powdered *wasabi*. The powder should be mixed with water to make a thick paste. *Wasabi* accompanies most *sashimi* dishes, and also *Sushi*. *Sashimi* may be hard to try for the first time, but with the added taste of soy sauce and *wasabi*, it will become one of your favorites.

YUBA(FILMY CURD OF SOYBEAN MILK)

Yuba, a treasured delicacy from Kyoto, is the skin formed on the surface of soybean milk in the process of making *tofu*. It is usually sold in dried sheets or small swirls and is used as a wrapper for rolled food or a soup ingredient.

YUZU CITRON

Japanese citron. The fragrant rind is grated and added as a garnish to soups and other dishes. This citrus fruit appears also in Chinese and Korean cooking. In the West where *yuzu* citron is not often available, lemon or lime rind or zest can be used though neither is quite the same.